DIVINE PRINCIPLES

DIVINE PRINCIPLES

Updated Edition   Robert McClurkin

PUBLISHER'S NOTE
Much of the ministry contained in this volume has appeared
as articles in UPLOOK (formerly ASSEMBLY ANNALS) during the past two years with a heartening response of reader
appreciation. Herein there is not only ample truth to enable
the honest seeker after the Lord to find Him and His "so great,
salvation," but also milk for children under instruction and
strong meat for the young men and the fathers in the family
of God. It is with pleasure that we commend this book to the
reader (February, 1970).

DIVINE PRINCIPLES
By: Robert McClurkin
Copyright © 2010
GOSPEL FOLIO PRESS
All Rights Reserved

Published by
GOSPEL FOLIO PRESS
304 Killaly St. W.
Port Colborne, ON L3K 6A6
CANADA

ISBN: 978-1-926765-15-0

Cover design by Lisa Martin
All Scripture quotations from the
King James Version unless otherwise noted.

Printed in USA

Contents

Foreword

At the request of my beloved brother and fellow-labourer in the Gospel, Robert McClurkin, it is my pleasure to commend the following pages to all of the Lord's people who gather unto His precious name. Having read the manuscripts before going to press, I am convinced they are the result of a deep and prayerful exercise of heart on the part of the writer. While these truths have been set forth both in oral and written ministry for many years, many of us feel the need of having them re-emphasized in this present day. I feel confident that the desire of the author is stated in the words of 2 Peter 1:12, *"Wherefore I will not be negligent to put you always in remembrance of these things; though ye know them, and be established in the present truth."* May this book be read in the spirit of the admonition of Hebrews 2:1, *"Therefore we might to give the more earnest heed to the things which we have heard, lest at any time we should let them slip."*

In a day of increasing carelessness and liberalism there is the danger of treating far too lightly these precious truths that have been taught and held so dearly by those who love and appreciate God's divine gathering centre. With the rapid and dangerous growth of organization, the widespread solicitation of emphasis placed on intellectualism and professionalism to the detriment of that which is spiritual and the alarming and unscriptural trend toward interdenominationalism, the very foundation of our assembly testimony is being threatened.

Let us face the challenge presented in Genesis chapters 11 and 12. Will it be *"the tower"* and *"let us make us a name"* or will it be *"the tent"* — the sign of our pilgrimage and the place where God reveals Himself at the altar in sweet communion, in the light of which the glory of this world fades away? As *"we go forth unto Him without the camp,"* we have a spiritual heritage to pursue. We are called out of the world and put out of touch with its false ways that we may be put in touch with the Almighty and His order of things in Christ, ever hearing and heeding His Word, *"Behold, I come quickly: hold that fast which thou hast, that no man take thy crown"* (Rev. 3:11).

—GORDON M. REAGER

Preface

THOSE WHO GATHER IN THE LORD'S NAME ALONE

WHAT THEY BELIEVE

This small book is written for the purpose of guiding the saints into the right ways of the Lord. In spite of the increased religious confusion, *"there is a path which no fowl knoweth, and which the vulture's eye hath not seen"* (Job 28:7). It is a path marked out by the Word of God and discerned by faith alone.

The Christians who meet in divine simplicity believe that Christ and Christ alone is the one divine gathering centre of the people of God. For that reason they reject all denominational tags as inconsistent with the New Testament pattern. They believe that the children of God are members of the one Body of Christ which is the one and only true Church of the living God. In harmony with the divine pattern they will only accept those scriptural names that embrace the whole Church. Four of these names are given to us in the Acts of the Apostles: Believers, Brethren, Disciples and Christians. These names link themselves with the four aspects of the devotional life of the church in chapter two: as believers they continued in the apostles' doctrine; as brethren they continued in the fellowship; as disciples they continued in the breaking of bread, or weekly celebration of the Lord's supper; as Christians they continued in prayers for the lost around them. Thus the grace of God transformed their lives and made them lovers of the Word of God, lovers of the people of God, lovers of the Christ of God and lovers of the souls of men who were exposed to the wrath of God.

The basis is now formed for a true scriptural fellowship where the saints can meet and enjoy all their spiritual privileges as well as share in the spiritual responsibilities. Indeed, it is incumbent upon all believers to accept God's divine order for the collective gatherings of His people and to allow the Word of God to guide and control in every devotional exercise. To save Israel from religious confusion, God commanded that collectively they were to meet only where "the Lord had placed His Name." The authority of God would then be supreme in all their religious exercises. The Name of our Lord is linked with the local assembly in Matthew 18. This is for the very same purpose, that His authority will be supreme in the assemblies of the saints.

Like the large upper room in Mark 14 where the Lord, with His disciples, introduced the remembrance feast, the place where He is pleased to put His Name is selected, secluded and elevated above the world and all its ways. It is a large place — large enough for all the people of God who will follow the divine order of the New Testament. It is large enough for all the Word of God, for the exercise of all spiritual gifts and for the sovereignty of the divine Spirit to use these gifts as He pleases. It was a nameless place. Of this upper room we read that it was "furnished and prepared." In that statement the Spirit of God would remind us that where our Lord meets with His own there is no place for human innovation or organization. It is fully furnished with a variety of gift to meet the variety of need among the saints.

In these assemblies of the Lord's people patterned after the divine order there is no room for the exclusive one-man ministry nor for the every-man ministry. Neither the cleric nor the unprofitable talker has any place in God's simple order. But each member has the liberty to function according to the ability that God has given him.

DOCTRINAL BELIEFS

These believers who seek to meet according to the New Testament pattern are fundamental in every way and true to "the historic faith of God's elect." To mention but a few things that are basic and essential in the fabric of true Christianity:

1. They believe in the absolute accuracy and verbal inspiration of Holy Scripture (2 Tim. 3:16; 2 Pet. 1:21). Mr. A. J. Pollock sums up our convictions concerning the perfections of the Word of God in these words:

> Five passages may be cited to prove without doubt the verbal perfection of our Bible (Heb. 12:27; John 10:34-36; Gal. 3:16; 4:9; John 8:58). In the first passage the argument turns on the significance of a single phrase; in the second on the inviolability of a single word, in the third on the use of a singular instead of a plural, in the fourth on the passive instead of the active voice of a verb, in the fifth on the use of the present instead of the past tense of a verb. Taking the five together we are taught that the Scripture cannot be broken, so far as to change a phrase, a word, the number of a noun, or the voice or tense of a verb.

> Whence but from heaven could men,
>   unskilled in arts,
> In several ages born in several parts,
>   weave such agreeing truths,
> Or how or why should all conspire to cheat us
>   with a lie,
> Unasked their pains, ungrateful their advice,
> Starving their gain and martyrdom
>   their price.

2. They believe that there is one true God whose radiant love flows through three distinct Personalities. The Father emphasizes the essence of the divine nature; the Son, the manifestation of that nature; and the Spirit, the operations of that nature (Matt. 28:19; 2 Cor. 13:14). Each is equal in substance and power and each possesses exclusively the attributes of Deity which are omnipotence, omniscience and omnipresence. Each is eternal in His existence,

divine in His nature and distinct in His personality. Not three Gods but one, for *"the LORD our God is one LORD"* (Duet. 6:4). Yet this is a compound unity. The Godhead is One in essence, power, glory and purpose, yet is expressed in the three distinct Pesonalities whose wills are never in conflict because they move from the purest motives and from the highest moral and spiritual virtues, the perfection of which alone is resident in Deity.

3. They believe that the Lord Jesus Christ is the eternal Son of God, miraculously born in time of the virgin Mary. The incarnation of the Son of God brought into union two natures, the human and the divine. Through these His one unique personality was revealed. In assuming perfect humanity, the Son of God became what He never was before, a man, yet He never ceased to be what He always was, God. Truly God was manifest in flesh (1 Tim. 3:16). As Son of God He could reach the throne, and as the Son of Man He could reach us. He was the true Jacob's ladder that touched both heaven and earth. Then at the cross He laid the foundation for the reconciliation of man to God (John 1:1-3; Phil. 2:5-11; Col. 1:15-18; Heb. 1).

> Like man, He walked; like God, He talked;
> His words were oracles,
>   His deeds were miracles;
> Of God, the best expression; of man,
>   the finest specimen;
> Full orbed humanity, crowned with Deity,
> No taint of iniquity, no trace of infirmity,
> ECCE-HOMO—behold the Man!
> ECCE-DEUS—behold thy God!

4. They believe that the Holy Spirit is a divine Person who, on the ascension of Christ to Heaven in all the virtue of accomplished redemption, came down to take up His abode in the Church. He works not only in His own divine sovereignty, but also through the members of the Body of Christ to spread the knowledge of God in the world. He presides over the exercise of gift in the church. He is the oil for the lamp of our testimony and the power to live for God against all opposition.

5. They believe that man is ruined by the fall and corrupted by sin and therefore unfit for heaven. Man's degradation is a revelation of his lost condition and his helplessness to save himself. Therefore salvation must be by grace alone (Rom. 3:23; Eph. 2:8,9; Titus 3:5).

Thus they believe that on the cross Christ fully paid the penalty for sin by dying *"the just for the unjust, that He might bring us to God"* (1 Peter 3:18). His blood alone is God's remedy for man's ruin and cleanses from all sin the soul that receives Him as Saviour and Lord (John 1:12; Rom. 10:9; 1 Jn. 1:7).

6. They believe that God fully accepted the propitiation or atonement made by the death of His Son by raising Him from the dead and setting Him at His own right hand to be a Prince and a Saviour (1 Cor. 15:17-20; Rom. 4:25; Acts 2:32) .

7. They believe that on man's part the sinner must repent and receive Christ as a personal Saviour. This results in a new birth (John 3) and the merits of the atonement being reckoned to him (John 3:16; 5:24; Acts 16:31).

The true Gospel and the only Gospel may be summed up in four great statements: Ruin by the fall, Redemption by blood, Regeneration by the Spirit and Responsibility of the sinner to accept or reject its message.

8. They believe that between death and resurrection there is an intermediate state in which the disembodied spirits of all await the resurrection. At death all who have accepted and all who die under the years of responsibility go to heaven. All who reject Him go to hell (2 Cor. 5:1-8; Phil. 1:23; Ps. 9:17; Luke 16:23).

9. They believe that there will be a resurrection of both the just and the unjust. The first takes place at the second advent of Christ, who will raise the dead who have died in Christ and change the living saints. Both will be caught up together to meet the Lord in the air. This is called the first resurrection and the rapture (John 14:3; 1 Cor. 15:51-58; 1 Thess. 4:13-18; Rev. 20:4).

The second takes place at the end of the one thousand years' reign of Christ on earth. Then the wicked dead will be raised to face the judgement of the great white throne. The books will be opened and the dead shall be judged according to the things recorded of their deeds on earth. The awful sentence will be passed. All whose names were not written in the Lamb's book of life will be cast into the lake of fire. This is the second death, an eternal separation from God (John 5:28, 29; Acts 17:31; Rev. 20:11-15).

10. They believe that the coming of the Lord may be at any moment. It will be pre-millennial and in two stages. In the first stage He will receive from the world His own, both dead and living, to meet Him in the air. In the second stage He will come with all His saints, in flaming fire, to take vengeance on the ungodly and to set up His Kingdom on earth. During this Millennium the Devil will be bound in the bottomless pit while the Prince of Peace will spread righteousness from shore to shore (Isa. 11; 35; 66; Rev. 19).

After the Millennium the Devil will be loosed for a little season and will stir up man (unsaved man) to his last rebellion against God. A rebellion, the guilt of which will be aggravated in the light of the love and grace that they witnessed during the Lord's benevolent reign. The human material on which he will work will be those who have rejected the Prince of Peace. Judgement will fall upon them from heaven. Then the great white throne will be set up where the wicked dead will be judged. This is the last event in time when death and hell will be cast into the lake of fire. Thus ends the great parenthesis which we call time. Death, the last enemy will then be destroyed. The great eternal state will begin where sin will be no more. It is the substance of the typical "morrow after the sabbath," the "eighth day," the new beginning when Christ will deliver up the kingdom to the Father, and God (the Triune God) shall be all in all.

> May He who from the vanquished grave
> The great, good Shepherd brought,
> Who rolled back death's terrific tide
> And full redemption wrought;
> Perfect Thy saints in every grace
> Till that bright day shall come,
> When we shall see Him face to face
> In our eternal home.

PSALM 19

7 The law of the Lord is perfect, converting the soul: the testimony of the Lord is sure, making wise the simple.

8 The statutes of the Lord are right, rejoicing the heart: the commandment of the Lord is pure, enlightening the eyes.

9 The fear of the Lord is clean, enduring forever: the judgements of the Lord are true and righteous altogether.

10 More to be desired are they than gold, yea, than much fine gold: sweeter also than honey and the honeycomb.

11 Moreover by them is thy servant warned: and in keeping of them there is great reward.

12 Who can understand his errors? Cleanse thou me from secret faults.

13 Keep back thy servant also from presumptuous sins; let them not have dominion over me: then shall I be upright, and I shall be innocent from the great transgression.

14 Let the words of my mouth, and the meditation of my heart, be acceptable in thy sight, O Lord, my strength and my redeemer.

1

The New Life in Christ our Lord

From the moment you trusted the Lord Jesus Christ as the Saviour of sinners you were brought under the shelter of the blood of His atonement. It is that blood that makes you safe for ever while His Word makes you sure. What a security is yours and what a consolation to know you are fitted for heaven by the work of our glorious Redeemer. Goodness and mercy will now follow you all the days of your life (Ps. 23). These two words have their exposition in the epistle to the Romans. It is the goodness of God that leadeth men to repentance (2:4) and it is the mercies of God that lead us to the full surrender of our all to Him (12:1, 2).

Having committed our souls to the saving and keeping power of our Lord, we are to learn the claims of the cross upon our entire being. The epistle to the Romans deals with four aspects of truth concerning the body of the believer. It describes what the body was before conversion, the servant of sin (6:12); it speaks of what the body is after conversion, the seat of a deadly conflict between the old and the new natures (7:24); it points to what the body will be in the future, changed and made like unto the glorious body of our Lord (8:11). The last aspect (12:1) indicates what the body should be now in the light of the mercies of God, a living sacrifice. It is the last aspect of this truth that we want to emphasize now.

There are three things in Romans twelve that we might note: a crisis as the result of the contemplation of the cross, the mercies of God; a transfiguration as the result of a process, the renewing of the mind; and an experience that leads to a sweet satisfaction, knowing the will of God.

17

1. The crisis. *"Your reasonable service"* is really "your priestly service." There is no doubt we have a reference here to the tribe of Levi in Numbers 8. Atonement was made for the Levites by the sin and burnt offerings (v. 12). In those offerings they saw the mercies of God making provision for their cleansing. Then when atonement was made, they themselves were made an offering unto the Lord, "that they might exercise the service of the Lord." The believer, like the Levite, contemplates the mercies of God as they flow from the one sacrifice of our glorious Lord. In the light of it he yields his body as a living sacrifice, "that he might do the service of the Lord." But, like the Levite, this priestly service is to be performed in fellowship with others. Note, there are many bodies but one sacrifice; variety is brought into unity. Then the chapter goes on to describe that unity expressed in variety of ministry (vv. 4-8).

This sacrifice is to be acceptable to God. In Malachi 1:8 we have sacrifice that was not acceptable to God. They offered the sick, the lame and the blind. Instead of sick, ours is to be holy; instead of lame, ours is to be acceptable; instead of blind, ours is to be intelligent — "your intelligent service." Prayers without feeling, service without enthusiasm and songs without heart are sickly devotions indeed, and an unthankful response to the mercies of God.

Crookedness in life and walk with the lame excuse that it is weakness, is dishonouring to the testimony and unacceptable to God.

What crimes have been committed in the name of the church! Blind religion has burned God's saints at the stake and tarnished the good names of noble men of God. We are to serve God with a mind enlightened by His truth. As the body is filled with the light of truth, the eye will be single for God's glory. Singleness of eye is not just sincerity, for we may be sincerely wrong, but sincerity directed by truth.

> Make sure of truth and truth will make
>   you sure,
> It will not shift, nor fade, nor die
> But like the heavens endure;

Man and his earth are changing day by day
Truth cannot change, nor ever grow feeble
or gray.

2. The transfiguration. As the crisis is brought about by the contemplation of the cross, the transfiguration is the result of beholding the glory that shines in the face of our exalted Lord (2 Cor. 3:18). It is interesting to note that the word *"changed"* is the same word that is translated *"transformed"* in Romans and *"transfigured"* in Matthew 17. Thus, in the only three places in the New Testament where this word is found, we have the Pattern of our transfiguration — the Lord Jesus Christ (Matt. 17:2), the Principle of it (Rom. 12:2) — the renewing of the mind, and the Power of it — even as by the Spirit of the Lord (2 Cor. 3:18).

3. The experience. It is proving the will of God. As we see diversity brought into unity in verse one, so in verses four to eight we see that unity brought into diversity. There are many members, each with his own work to do and all complement each other. Free-lances and independents are not contemplated. The will of God is that we may walk and work with the local assembly of which we form a part.

Now the question may arise, "What is the niche that I may fill? Where will I function for God?" Note the variety of gift in the local assembly here where there is divine liberty for the exercise of prophet, teacher, exhorter and overseer. Then if we are not in any of these categories there is ministry or service in general into which each of us may fit.

We have the body (v. 1), the mind (vv. 2, 3), the faculties (vv. 4-8) and the spirit in which all are to function (vv. 9-12). Study carefully in our chapter the purity of love (vv. 9-11), the activity of love, supplying the needs of others (vv. 11-15) and the humility of love (vv. 16-21). Thus truth, love, faith and humility are all brought into harmony through the surrendered lives of God's beloved people. What moral beauties of character are blended giving adornment to the testimony of God on earth.

Consider now the force of the word "present." It is a word that means to stand by, as a ship that goes to the rescue of another ship. It means "be ready for anything." Is this our attitude in the presence of God?

It denotes the presenting of a sacrifice, suggesting the full surrender of our all to God. Have we any reserve? Remember, God only guides what He governs.

It is used in connection with a court of law (2 Tim. 4:17) — *"the Lord stood by me."* Our surrender to God includes standing by the weak in defence of the truth. Do we let others bear the brunt of the conflict? Remember that divine truth has always been won and preserved by spiritual conffict.

It is used in Acts 23:24 to describe the provision that was made to carry Paul's belongings. Our love to God and to His people will ever lead us to be prepared to bear the burdens of others. This is the spirit that fulfills the law of Christ.

Are we ready for such a surrender? Let each of us search his own conscience and answer to God alone.

> True worth is being, not seeming,
> In doing each day that goes by
> Some little good — not in dreaming
> Of great things to do by and by:
> For whatever men say in blindness
> And spite of the fancies of youth,
> There's nothing so kingly as kindness
> And nothing so royal as truth.

2

Personality Equilibrium

Man in his original state was made in the image and likeness of God. Although the likeness of God was lost in the fall, the image still remains, though defaced by sin (Gen. 9:6). "Likeness" has the idea of resemblance, while "image" conveys the thought of representation. Professor Orr has pointed out three aspects of this image. He says,

> On our planet, man alone was made in the image of God. He was made in the rational image of God. He alone has the intelligence to understand the universe, the capacity to discover the cause and effect of all things.
>
> He was made in the moral image of God. Part of his constitution is the idea of God, the moral 'ought,' the ethical imperative, the possession of conscience which reveals moral law, a will to execute moral purposes and affections that create the capacity for moral love.
>
> He was made in the regal image of God. He is possessed with deputed sovereignty. This is seen in his conquests over nature and his employment of natural laws and forces to his own ends.
>
> The soul of man is the essence of personality and the seat of a double life, the corporal functions of physical life and the activities of the mind in the spiritual realm. The distinction between soul and spirit is a distinction within the one indivisible spiritual nature. The higher func-

tions of the spirit are also ascribed to the soul.

Man therefore in his fallen condition is like an heir dispossessed or like a prince dethroned and in disgrace. But God in His mercy devised means that His banished be not expelled from Him. Through the atoning death of His only Son a salvation is provided for man that restores the image and likeness of God to the soul. The *"new man,"* the born-again ego, is said to be *"after God created in righteousness and true holiness"* (Eph. 4:24). This salvation introduces man to an inheritance which is greater than what was lost in the fall (Col. 1:12; 1 Pet. 1:4), and by the power of the indwelling Spirit of God, it enables him to manifest the princely dignity of the new personality, reclaimed from the galling bondage of sin and Satan.

In the composition of man's complex being we must discern the difference between human nature and the flesh. Human nature is the creation of God. Flesh is that principle of sin which works in our members, debasing every taste of that nature and making it the slave of sin.

We must also discern the difference between the *"old man"* and *"the flesh."* The *"old man"* is the personality, the man in Adam, which was sentenced to death for sin. That sentence was executed on our Substitute, the Lord Jesus Christ, when He died on the cross. At conversion the *"new man"* emerges on the resurrection side of the cross, set free from death, to enjoy the freedom of the sons of God. That new personality is to be yielded to the will of God.

In this complex personality of man there is always the danger of imbalance. Physical monstrosities are repulsive. Personality monstrosities likewise repel. The first is pitiable; the second is contemptible. The first affects mainly itself; the second leaves its fingerprint on all it contacts.

There are at least four realms of human personality which must be developed in proper proportion. These are the Intellectual, the Emotional, the Physical and the Spiritual.

THE INTELLECTUAL

The mind of man thirsts for knowledge. This can only be perfectly satisfied with truth. God has placed no premium on ignorance. His oft repeated warning is, "Be not ignorant." Ignorance is the seed-plot of many bitter fruits. It engenders littleness of thought and leads to a contraction in the spheres of insight, outlook and ambition. It destroys the capacity for sound judgement and quenches the Spirit of knowledge and wisdom within us.

> Poor souls with stunted vision oft measure
> giants by their narrow gauge,
> The poisoned shafts of falsehood and derision
> are oft impelled against those who
> mold the age.

THE EMOTIONAL

The emotional part of our being, to be nourished properly, must be fed by that which draws out our sympathy and feelings for others. There has seldom been a day when there was so much emotional instability among us as now. The symptoms of this immaturity are manifest in the cruel tongue, the critical spirit and the crooked judgements which are coldly passed upon one another.

The emotions are to be fed by that which leads to an affinity of feeling in the joys and sorrows of others. The Bible says, *"Rejoice with them that do rejoice and weep with them that weep"* (Rom. 12:15). Our Lord's commendation to humble saints who finished their course with joy was this, *"For I was an hungered, and ye gave Me meat: I was thirsty, and ye gave Me drink: I was a stranger, and ye took Me in: naked, and ye clothed Me: I was sick and ye visited Me: I was in prison and ye came unto Me"* (Matt. 25:35-36). What was done for His people He counted done for Himself.

The Lord has graciously equipped us with the ability both to weep and to laugh. *"A merry heart doeth good like a medicine"* (Prov. 17:22). It is a well-known fact in the medical profession that there

23

are muscles in the face that are used in no other way except when we laugh. This emotional balance is decribed in the words of the wise man, there is *"A time to weep, and a time to laugh"* (Eccl. 3:4). Sanctified humour is a God-given quality of human personality. The Pharisees stifled this virtue and went down in history characterized by long robes, long prayers and long faces.

THE PHYSICAL

The body of redeemed man is the temple of the Holy Ghost. We are to glorify God in our bodies which are the Lord's. The Bible warns against the neglecting of the body (Col. 2:23). This was done by some who thought that the body was the seat, instead of the instrument of sin. Therefore they concluded that the guilty part must be punished by neglecting it. This folly is still practiced in many religious orders of today. But the Holy Spirit wants a healthy and vigorous body to work through whenever possible. When this is not possible, however, He can maintain a healthy state of soul within a weak body (3 Jn. 2). We are to present our bodies as a living sacrifice and yield our members as instruments of righteousness unto holiness.

To keep our body healthy there is a necessity for bodily exercise that *"profiteth for the little time we are here"* (1 Tim. 4:8). To neglect this leads to lethargy and laziness. This lack of physical energy hinders the Spirit of God from working through us in an energetic way.

There is also the danger of abuse as well as the neglecting of the body. The Bible warns against gluttony. There are also the habits of self-indulgence that impair health and shorten life. Let us not forget that the blood that flowed for sin purchased every part of our being, body, soul and spirit. Keep the temple of the Holy Ghost clean and healthy for the Lord. Not a few of the troubles among the people of God can be traced to a cantankerous spirit that is the direct result of a poor physical condition.

THE SPIRITUAL

The moment a sinner believes on the Lord Jesus Christ he is sprinkled by the blood from an evil conscience. This relieves him from the guilt of sin. But there is another cleansing that takes place; it is *"the washing of regeneration, and the renewing of the Holy Ghost"* (Tit. 3:5). This delivers him from the compulsion to sin. The latter has been called "the expulsive power of a new affection." A whole way of life has been displaced by a better and nobler way of life. This new life in Christ is nourished by prayer and the Word of God. As the new life is fed there will be an advancement in our knowledge of God and the will of God. Our love to God will grow and our intimacy with God will deepen through the years of our pilgrimage.

Now what are the dangers to the saints of God of neglecting to develop our personalities with balance and proportion? To feed the intellect at the expense of other areas of our being will result in an inflation of the ego, which instead of bringing the light of knowledge casts its shadow of superiority across the path of humble and gracious souls. This is a special danger in our day when intellectualism is displacing spirituality among us.

To surfeit the emotions to the starvation of the other departments of our being will produce a flabby sentimentalism that is devoid of strength of character and the fine balance of maturity.

To be obsessed with the care or the development of the physical to the detriment of the rest is to fall into the error of narcissism and to eclipse the spiritual growth of the personality which, in the natural process, is declining.

While the "new man" is constantly maintained and nurtured by the indwelling Spirit of God, as we abide in Christ, there are religious aspirations in human nature which, because of the principle of sin working in our members, ever seek to be gratified by externalisms. In the extreme this leads to monasticism. In its lesser degree it manifests itself in legalism and isolationism. This is the eccentricity which brought the anathema of our Lord down upon the heads of the scribes and Pharisees in His day. To feed the religious part of our being to the neglect of other parts will only result in self-righteous Pharisaism that is so repulsive to honest souls.

Equilibrium of personality is not only greatly to be desired in a Christian, but it is demanded of God. It is our intelligent service, to be yielded entirely to God to be moulded with proper balance in every part.

We have already pointed out from the book of Malachi that the people were offering to God that which was not acceptable to their governor. Could it be possible in our day that we could be guilty of the very same thing? We can think back only a few years ago of the sacrifices of blind religion offered in the Name of Christ on the racks of the Inquisition and the stakes of the martyrs. Perhaps closer to home we could find the remains of good reputations and noble names burnt to ashes in fire ignited by the tongues of some proclaiming allegiance, to the truth of God. Oh! the lameness of the excuses we offer to God for our lack of zeal and devotedness to Christ. With what poor hobbling steps do we seek to pursue a professedly sacrificial life for God. The Bible says, *"The legs of the lame are not equal"* (Prov. 26:7). What inequalities of justice, what unsound appraisals, what immoral principles are laid on the altar for God's approval. What revelations await us at the judgement seat of Christ!

The symptoms of spiritual sickness may be seen in the sleepiness of many prayer meetings, in the dull, half-hearted singing offered to God in the name of praise and in the lack of any enthusiasm in our service. Then to fill the vacuum left by a lack of the felt presence of God in our gatherings there is a demand to fill it with machinery. Religious entertainment then displaces the Word of God and God's people are amused instead of edified and led on in the ways of God and holiness. God give us spiritual equilibrium — that quality that will develop balanced lives for God. This will deliver us from reeling to extremes and enable us to walk a straight path with Christian dignity and poise.

> O may Thy Spirit guide our souls and
> mould them to Thy will,
> That from Thy paths we ne'er may stray,
> but keep Thy precepts still.

That to the Saviour's stature full we
    nearer still may rise,
And all we think, and all we do be pleasing
    in Thine eyes.

3

Eternal Security

God wants every believer to walk in the enjoyment of his possessions in Christ. When we receive the Lord Jesus Christ as Saviour and Lord, His atoning blood makes us safe and His infallible Word makes us sure. There are two statements of Christ in the gospels that contrast sharply. Of those who trust Him He says, *"I am the good shepherd, and know My sheep,"* (John 10:14). but of those who reject Him He says, *"I never knew you"* (Matt. 7:23). In the same chapter (John 10) He speaks in tender tones of the sheep that He knows and says, *"They shall never perish"* (John 10:28)

When the number of the redeemed is completed, our Lord, as the Firstborn, will say, *"Behold I and the children which God hath given Me,"* (Heb. 2:13). as much as to say, "Look them over and see, I have brought them all safely home." Of all whom the Father gave Him He will be able to say, *"I have lost none"* (John 18:9). The power that guards and keeps the saints of God enables the weakest to sing:

> Yes, I to the end shall endure
> as sure as the earnest is given,
> More happy but not more secure
> the glorified spirits in heaven.

Let us with joy and genuine appreciation to God look at the subject of the saints' preservation in four ways.

First, our security is assured by the nature of the new birth. This is a "once for all" experience. The expression "once and for all" in the original language is applied to the incarnation of

Christ (Heb. 9:26), to His sufferings (1 Pet. 3:18), to His death (Rom. 6:10; Heb. 7:27), to His victorious ascension (Heb. 9:12) and to the giving of the Scriptures to the saints (Jude 3) (see JND's translation). Is it not interesting to see the same expression applied to the believer's initial experience of trusting Christ, resulting in a "once and for all" enlightenment or illumination (Heb. 6:4; 10:32)? Our Lord impressed the same truth upon Peter when He said, *"He that is washed* (all over) *needeth not* (a repetition) *save to wash his feet, but is clean every whit"* (John 13:10). He was referring to the washing of regeneration as a *"once and for all"* experience. Our faith having been once put in Christ, the Son of God, not only brings about the new birth, but it brings us into the family of God (John 1:12; Gal. 3:26). This new birth can never be undone, nor can our relationship ever be severed. But someone may say, "What about the sins after we trust Christ?" Observe that the sins of God's people bring into activity the work of the Advocate, Jesus Christ the Righteous, who, on our confession, restores and forgives on the basis of the propitiation or atonement (1 Jn. 2:1-2). Note, too, that the advocate is with the Father, indicating that while sin breaks communion it does not alter relationship.

At the consecration of the Old Testament priests (Lev. 8), they were ceremonially bathed "once and for all." After that they only had to wash their hands and their feet at the laver. It is to that ritual that our Lord refers when He said, "He that is bathed needeth not, save to wash his feet only." The washing of the new birth needs no repetition, but we do need the daily application of the Word of God to cleanse our ways. As sinners we need the bath, as saints we need the basin (John 13:5). With respect to the truth of regeneration, the writer of the Hebrews (ch. 10) also refers to the ceremonial acts of Lev. 8, *"Having our hearts sprinkled from an evil conscience* (by the blood) *and our bodies washed with pure water"* (the washing of the new birth by the Word). The first is for the guilt of sin, the second is for the defilement of sin.

After the bathing in Lev. 8, the blood of the ram of consecration was applied to the ear, hand and foot. On top of the blood was put the holy anointing oil. Was Paul thinking of this when he said, *"Redeemed* (the blood) . . . *that we might receive the promise of the Spirit"* (Gal. 3:13-14) the oil on top of the blood? That means that the Spirit comes to indwell believers on the basis of the blood alone. He could no more leave us than the efficacy of the atonement should ever fail.

But the picture of the blood and oil on the ear, hand and foot would suggest that while we are saved by grace alone, *"We are bought with a price and we are not our own"* (1 Cor. 6:19-20). On the basis of the cross we claim salvation from the hand of God; on the basis of the same sacrifice God claims our bodies, souls and spirits as His own.

The application of the blood and oil to the ear would suggest that God now claims our attention. This affects our personalities. The application to the thumb suggests our grasp and would therefore affect our possessions. The application to the great toe would suggest our balance and would thus affect our path. In other words, all that we are and have belongs to God.

Second, our security is assured by the promises of God. Is eternal life a gift (Rom. 6:23)? Then *"the gifts and callings of God are without repentance"* (Rom. 11:29). We are begotten unto an inheritance that is reserved for us and we are preserved for the inheritance (1 Pet. 1:3-5). We are kept *"to be presented before the presence of His glory with exceeding joy"* (Jude 24). By the love of His heart and the might of His hand we are to be preserved unto the end for He loves us to the uttermost and He saves to the uttermost (John 13:1; Heb. 7:25). All His saints are in His hands and no enemy can pluck the weakest from the hand of omnipotence (Deut. 33:3; John 10:28, 29). It is eternal life He gives us and that life is hid with Christ in God (Col. 3:3). Who could ever steal it away? In Romans 8 Paul seems to anticipate every enemy that would try. There are the demands of Justice. But *"who can lay a charge against God's elect? It is God that justifies"* (vv. 31-34). There is the adversity of circumstances (vv. 35-37). Note the seven scattering weapons in verse 35 with which the Devil takes the offensive against the Lord's people. But not one of these can separate us from the love of Christ. That love is strong as death; it holds tenaciously to its object and will not give it up. Then there are the forces of the universe (vv. 38, 39). Though he scans the universe, all creatures that he knows about could not destroy the weakest saint. Then he says, "Nor any other creature." Should there be any other creatures in God's far-flung universe, even they could not separate us from the love of God which is in Christ Jesus our Lord.

Why is Paul, by the Spirit, so sure about it? Notice a little phrase used three times in the chapter, *"FOR US."* God is for us in justification (v. 31). Christ is for us in acceptance (v. 34). The Spirit is for us in intercession (vv. 26,27).

Notice another expression that is used three times in the chapter: *"ALL THINGS."* All things are working together for our good (v. 28). All things are freely given unto us (v. 32). All things are subdued before us (v. 37). No wonder he says in triumph, *"Nay, in all these things we are more than conquerors through Him that loved us"* (Rom. 8:37). There can be no condemnation (v. 1), no accusation (v. 34), and no separation (v. 35) to them who are in Christ Jesus our Lord.

> Grace will complete what grace begins,
> To save from sorrow or from sins:
> The work that Wisdom undertakes
> Eternal mercy ne'er forsakes.

Third, our security is assured by the Blood of the Lamb. It is called *"the blood of the everlasting covenant"* (Heb. 13:20). By virtue of His death, our Lord is the Author of an *"eternal salvation,"* and *"eternal redemption"* and an *"eternal inheritance"* (Heb. 5:9; 9:12-14) Finality is stamped upon the work of God's saving grace in the three "no mores" in Hebrews 10. So far as Christ is concerned there will be *"no more offering for sin"* (v. 18). So far as God is concerned there will be *"no more remembrance of sin"* (v. 17). So far as we are concerned there will be *"no more conscience of sin"* (v. 2)—that is, in the sense of penal retribution. Thus, by virtue of the blood of the Lamb, God puts our sins out of reach (Psa. 103:12), out of sight (Isa. 38:17) and out of mind (Heb. 10:17). That blood that made our peace with God (Col. 1:20), that cleanses from all sin (1 Jn. 1:7) and forever looses us from sin's penalty (Rev. 1:5), abides eternally in its efficacy for the people of God. Fourth, our security is assured by the high priestly ministry of Christ. *"For if when we were enemies we were reconciled to God by the death of His Son, much more being reconciled, we shall be saved by His life"* (Rom. 5:10)—the risen life of our glorious Lord. He who loves to the uttermost, saves to the uttermost, that is, the uttermost length of time. From the moment we put our trust in Him until we reach the Father's home, we have a Saviour the whole way home.

How does Christ save us daily by His life? He saves us daily by the prayer of that risen life (Luke 22:31, 32; Heb. 9:24). He saves us daily by the power of that risen life. He is able to keep that which was committed unto Him against that day (2 Tim. 1:12). No foe can defeat His purposes to save us unto the end.

> When I fear my faith will fail
> Christ will hold me fast;
> When the tempter would prevail
> Christ will hold me fast.

He saves us daily by the perpetuity of that risen life. As the man-slayer was safe in the city of refuge so long as the high priest lived, so we have fled for refuge to Christ who is our city of refuge. He is also our great High Priest who is alive for evermore. He said, *"Because I live, ye shall live also"* (John 14:19).

He saves us daily by the promises of that risen life. We are saved in hope. The indwelling Spirit of God is the seal that marks the property of God on earth (Eph. 1:13). That seal *"is unto the day of redemption"* (Eph. 4:30). His presence in each believer is the guarantee of our glorification in the day of our Lord's return (Rom. 8:11).

> The Shepherd's bosom bears each lamb
> o'er rock and waste and wild;
> The object of that love I am
> and carried like a child.

Divine and sovereign grace alone will mark the salvation of God in all its aspects. As to salvation from the judgement of sin we read, *"For by grace are ye saved through faith;"* (Ephesians 2:8) as to salvation from the power of sin we read, *"My grace is sufficient for thee;"* (2 Cor. 12:9) as to the salvation from the presence of sin we read, *"Be sober, and hope to the end for the grace that is to be brought unto you at the revelation of Jesus Christ"* (1 Peter 1:13).

> The work which His goodness began,
> The arm of His strength will complete,
> His promise is yea and amen
> And never was forfeited yet.
>
> Things future nor things that are now,
> Not all things below or above
> Can make Him His purpose forego,
> Or sever my soul from His love.

4

Christian Baptism

There is a beautiful simplicity to the divine order of the New Testament. If we keep to this order there will be no confusion. Confusion regarding baptism resulted from the introduction of baby-sprinkling and, later on, of household baptism, which is the immersion of babies. Neither of these innovations is true to the practice of the New Testament nor to the truth that baptism is designed to set forth.

The word "baptize" means to dip or submerge. As the symbol of burial it suggests to cover completely. But we can only bury what is already dead (the old man). The sprinkling or immersion of babies is a contradiction of that truth. It is more: it is an error, the fruit of which has undermined the principles of the true Gospel of our Lord Jesus Christ.

Believer's baptism alone is taught in the Word of God. It is commanded in the Gospels, practiced in the Acts, and explained in the Epistles. It lies at the door of salvation and is meant to be a public testimony to our death, burial and resurrection with Christ (Rom. 6:3-4). In Matthew 28 the responsibility to see that the young converts are baptized is on the evangelist, whereas in Mark 16 that responsibility is on the converts. If this principle is observed there will be no problem of unbaptized believers in assembly fellowship. This will not make baptism a door into the assembly. We meet with it before we reach that door.

Let us look at the subject of baptism in three ways:

I. WHY SHOULD BELIEVERS BE BAPTIZED?

First, because as children of God we are already baptized in the Holy Ghost, a baptism that became effective the moment we believed. Think for a moment what it means: it is a baptism into Christ (Gal. 3:27), that is into vital union with Christ. It is a baptism into His death (Rom. 6:3), that is into all the value of His atonement. It is a baptism into the Body of Christ (1 Cor. 12:13), that is into vital relationship with all the Lord's people. Water baptism is the God-given symbol to show this forth. God does not separate the two. The one is the symbol of the other. Much argument and confusion has resulted from trying to divorce them. Some argue that such Scripture passages as Romans 6:3, Galatians 3:27 and Ephesians 4:5 refer to our baptism in the Spirit. Others say they refer to our baptism in water. The logical interpretation is that they refer to both water and Spirit baptism. The one is the symbol of the other, "the outward seal of an inward work divine."

Second, we should be baptized because God commands it (Matt. 28:19; Acts 10:47, 48). Love to the Lord Jesus Christ will always manifest itself in obedience (John 14:15). In fact this is the first step of obedience in a life well-pleasing to God. Let us always remember, too, that when we respond to each revelation of truth it leads to a deeper enrichment of our spiritual lives and a greater vision of the will of God.

> Not in dumb resignation we lift our hands
>   on high,
> Not like the nerveless fatalist, content to do
>   or die;
> Our faith springs like the eagle
>   who soars to meet the sun
> And cries exulting unto Thee,
>   "O Lord, Thy will be done."

Third, we should be baptized because it is the Christian's privilege to make a public testimony to the truth of our death, burial and resurrection with Christ.

2. WHO ARE TO BE BAPTIZED?

The answer of the Bible is: believers only (Acts 2:41; 8:12,36-38; 9:18; 10:47,48; 18:8; 19:4,5). A careful reading of the Acts will show that believers only were baptized on confession of their faith in Christ (8:37). The simple order of God is, *"They (the Corinthians) hearing, believed and were baptized"* (18:8). If the Scriptures do not anticipate an unbaptized believer, why should we look upon baptism as a non-essential? It is not essential to get into heaven, we know, for many unbaptized believers will be there. But surely it is essential to the path of faith, Again, why should an assembly receive unbaptized believers when there is none found in the assemblies of the New Testament? Does the order of God in His Holy Word mean nothing to us? The practice of the early church points to a straight course for us to follow.

3. WHAT IS THE SIGNIFICANCE OF BAPTISM?

This holy ordinance of God sets forth many lessons for God's people to learn:

a. It is a public renunciation. *"But ye have washed yourselves"* (1 Cor. 6:11, proper translation). The only other place where a similar expression is used is Acts 22:16, *"Arise and be baptized and wash away thy sins."* Saul's sins had been forgiven three days before. What did such a command mean? It simply meant that in his baptism, as in ours, there is a public renunciation of our old life in Adam. We are dead and buried to it all. We have now a new resurrection life to be lived for God.

b. it is an initiation. At the moment of our conversion we were baptized in the Spirit by our Lord. This introduced us to a new world of spiritual delights. Paul refers to this when he says, *"Ye are not in the flesh but in the Spirit"* (Rom. 8:9.) Positionally we have been immersed into the realm where the Spirit is Lord. It is that heavenly sphere of infinite peace and joy where

> Heaven above is softer blue,
> earth around is sweeter green,
> Something lives in every hue

that Christless eyes have never seen;
Birds with gladder songs o'erflow,
flowers with deeper beauties shine,
Since I know as now I know,
that I am His and He is mine.

c. It is an identification. Water baptism sets forth our identification with our Lord in His death, burial and resurrection
(Rom. 6:3-5). In His death we received the judgement our sins
deserved. Our "old man" was crucified with Christ. In His
burial we see ourselves cut off from the world where once we
found our pleasure and satisfaction. This is the world which
still rejects our blessed Lord and whose pleasure depends on
the exclusion of God. In His resurrection we see ourselves rise
to newness of life. Just as Israel's baptism in the Red Sea was
unto Moses, which meant unto new leadership, so we leave
the bondage of sin and slavery behind us to follow our rejected
Lord, the Leader and Commander of His beloved people (Heb.
2:10; 12:2).

Who points the clouds their course, whom winds
and sea obey, He shall direct thy wandering feet,
He shall prepare thy way.

d. It is an anticipation. *"Else what shall they do who are baptized for the dead* (with reference to the dead, which seems to be
the meaning), *if the dead rise not"* (1 Cor. 15:29). It does not mean
being baptized for somebody already dead. Scripture knows
nothing of such a practice. It means rather being baptized in
reference to the dead that they shall rise again. Baptism has no
significance if there be no resurrection from the dead. Just as
our spirits have risen to new resurrection life (Col. 3:1), so our
baptism teaches us that our bodies will rise in resurrection glory to a grand immortality where sin will be no more.

In conclusion we would repeat for emphasis what is taught
in 1 Corinthians about this important subject: The ordinance of
baptism is carried out by the authority of Christ (1:13); it is a
public renunciation of sinful living (6:11); it is unto new Leader-

ship (10:2) and it is a witness to the resurrection to life of all who have fallen asleep through Jesus (15:29).

> Salvation's Captain and our Guide of all that
> seek the rest above;
> Beneath Thy shadow we abide, the cloud of
> Thy protecting love.

Our strength, Thy grace; our rule, Thy Word; our end, the glory of the Lord.

5

Gathering in His Name

"For where two or three are gathered together in My Name, there am I in the midst of them" (Matt. 18:20).

The Gospel according to Matthew may be divided into seven parts. The first part introduces us to the King. The seven witnesses who are brought forward to testify of His greatness leave us in no doubt that He was none less than "God manifest in the flesh." The witnesses are: the witness of history in His genealogy (1:1-17), of the angels at His birth (1:18-21), of the star that guided the wise men (2: 1-11), of the Scriptures of truth (1:22; 2:5, 17,23), of John the Baptist, His forerunner (3:1-12), of the Father at His baptism (3:13-17), and of the Holy Spirit at His temptation (4:1). The last part describes His atoning death and victorious resurrection. Between the first and last parts we have five great discourses of our Lord, each ending in almost exactly the same words, *"when Jesus had made an end of these sayings"* (7:28, 11:1, 13:53, 19:1, 26:1). In these discourses we have:

Chapters 5 -7	The Teacher imparting His own character to His disciples
Chapter 10	The Master revealing the principles of Christian service
Chapter 13	The King enlightening His subjects to the character of the dispensation
Chapter 18	The Head controlling the members in happy church relationship
Chapters 24 & 25	The Judge calling His creatures to account when the age has run its course

It is the fourth great discourse that demands our attention now. Matthew 18 has four beautiful pictures of character that are to adorn the local churches of the saints. In these we have the unity of a common relationship—a child in the family (vs. 1-11); the unity of a common attraction—a sheep in the flock (vs. 12-14); the unity of common values—a brother in the assembly (vs. 15-20); the unity of a common attitude—a servant in the kingdom (vs. 21-35). In these pictures we have four aspects of the spirit of the kingdom of heaven which is really the spirit of Christ. They are: the spirit of humility—the child; of godly care—the Shepherd; of peace—the brother; of brotherly forgiveness—the servant.

1. THE UNITY OF A COMMON RELATIONSHIP

At this time the disciples had been disputing as to who should be the greatest. In striving for the masteries they had lost the victory in the valley (ch. 17). Our Lord put the child in their midst to teach them that true greatness in the kingdom of heaven is advancement in the spirit of Christ. He had said in chapter eleven, *"Learn of Me for I am meek and lowly in heart and ye shall find rest unto your souls."* In that child they saw the picture of innocence, humility, trust and unconscious virtue. Someone has said that "the higher grades of greatness are rewards of childlikeness." Childlikeness is not childishness. Paul makes the distinction in these words, *"In malice be children, in understanding be men."*

So precious to the Lord is the childlike believer that He gives a solemn warning against offending him. In the context He says, *"Let there be nothing in the hand* (what we do), *or in the foot* (where we go), *or in the eye* (what we plan), *that would deliberately offend or injure the humble among the saints."* He who habitually hurts such would, in his persistent course of evil, prove himself to be but a wicked servant whose destiny is the outer darkness forever (vs. 8, 9). Humble saints are not left to defend themselves. Our Lord speaks of the guardianship of angels. Not only are these assigned to the special charge of protecting them, but they have access to the presence of the Father to lay a charge against any who would do them injury (v. 10), or swiftly strike down their adversary (Acts 12:23).

The assembly of God is to be adorned by the grace of humility. It is the soil in which every other Christlike virtue grows.

> The bird that soars on highest wing builds in
> the ground her lowly nest,
> While she who does most sweetly sing,
> sings in the shade when all things rest;
> In lark and nightingale we see,
> what honour hath humility.

2. THE UNITY OF A COMMON ATTRACTION

Sheep, while attracted to the shepherd, are prone to wander. If one of Christ's sheep wanders, the whole flock suffers, for what is a reproach to one is a reproach to all. Our Shepherd has placed a value upon each sheep. If one goes astray He will leave no stone unturned to seek its recovery. He knoweth His own sheep by name. Ezekiel describes the shepherd-heart of God in chapter 34 of that book: "As a shepherd seeketh out his flock . . . so will I seek My sheep in all places where they have been scattered" (v. 12). What a contrast to those who took the place of under shepherds! There is a strong indictment in the first six verses that should put the fear of God into every professed leader among the saints today. "Woe be to the shepherds of Israel that do feed themselves! Should not the shepherds feed the flocks? The diseased have ye not strengthened, neither have ye healed that which is sick, neither have ye bound up that which is broken, neither have ye brought again that which was driven away, neither have ye sought that which was lost. But with force and with cruelty have ye ruled them and they were scattered." Oh! to feel the burden of the sheeps' wanderings and the reproach of their sin. So many of us have not learned to eat part of the sin offering in the holy place when we feel the grief of a brother's fall (Gal. 6:1, 2). God give us men who will feed and lead the flock with the compassion of Christ.

Oh give us hearts to love like Thine,
    like Thee, O Lord, to grieve,
Far more for others' sins than all the wrongs
    that we receive.
One with Thyself may every eye in us,
    Thy brethren, see
That gentleness and grace that springs
    from union, Lord, with Thee.

3. UNITY OF COMMON VALUES

The word *"Brethren"* is a lovely word. Almost its first appearance in the Bible is in Genesis 13, *"Let there be no strife . . . for we be brethren."* The true value of this relationship is learned only in fellowship with Christ. In one of its last appearances we read, *"Love as brethren."* The procedure developed in verses 15 to 20 must be in the spirit of the kingdom of heaven. Otherwise it will not be acknowledged by God. Only what is bound by the Word of God on earth will be bound by the will of God in heaven. It has been truly said, "If through error or envy any one be cast out of the church, Christ will find that soul in mercy" J.A.M. (cf. John 9:34,35).

The offence here is not just a mere difference of opinion. It is serious enough to disturb the fellowship of all. It must be put right. There are a few salutary lessons we all may learn: First, the action taken against the offending brother must be carried out in the spirit of Christ. This we have indicated is the spirit of humility, of godly care, the spirit of peace and of brotherly forgiveness.

Second, the emphasis in all this procedure is to gain thy brother. It is not a battle to win an argument, but an endeavor to win a brother. Both the offended and the offending will lose if reconciliation is not effected.

Third, we are not to make a public dispute out of something that is of a private character. The church, that is the local church, is not brought in except as a last extremity. One could not refer a matter like this to the universal church. Our Lord is anticipating the universal church expressing itself in what is called "the churches of the saints." Each was to be a miniature of the one great whole.

Fourth, the offending brother who refuses to be won back must be prepared to go through life out of fellowship with God and with His people. He puts himself in the place of the heathen man or publican, which is outside the assembly. However, we must strive for the restoration of the offending brother as we would for the salvation of the heathen and the publican. This godly exercise has bound his sin upon him and will only be loosed upon his repentance. He has excommunicated himself. Incidently, the word "loosed" which is seen again in verse 27, is contingent upon repentance. God does not forgive the impenitent, nor does He ask His people to do so.

4. THE UNITY OF A COMMON ATTITUDE

The Father's daily forgiveness of us, His children, is only assured when we possess the spirit of brotherly forgiveness towards others. The brother who goes through life with an unforgiving spirit will usually end his life in the hands of the tormentors (v. 34). We have lived long enough to see hard and unforgiving men end their lives in this way. Some have died without the comforts of the Word of God. Others without the assurance of salvation. Even the sweet anticipation of heaven and home was denied them. May God help us to keep in fellowship with God and to cultivate a sweet Christlike spirit until we see Him face to face.

It is in this context that verse 20 is set. *"For where two or three are gathered together in My Name, there am I in the midst of them."* Let us see in this verse the sweet simplicity of God's assembly, functioning in the spirit of the kingdom of heaven.

a. Its unity. There is a song in verse 19. The word *"agree"* has a musical connotation. Wherever saints are willing to meet in subjection to the risen Head of the church, the music of heaven will have come down to earth. A colony of heaven will be planted in that locality.

b. Its locality — where? Anywhere a company of the Lord's people meet in His Name alone and in accordance with His holy Word, there we may behold the simplicity of the New Testament church.

> A church, what is it? A band of faithful men
> Met for God's worship in some humble room,
> > on hillside or lone glen,
> To hear the counsels of His holy Word,
> > pledged to each other
> And their common Lord, these,
> > few as they may be
> Compose the church, such as in pristine
> > age defied the tyrant's steel,
> The bigot's rage, for where but two or three
> > whate'er their place—
> In faith's communion meet,
> There, with Christ present, is a church
> > complete.

c. Its centre. "Together in My Name." In this connection there are three Scriptures that blend most beautifully. In these we see the Principle, the Command and the Promise in relation to the gathering together of the saints in assembly capacity. In Genesis 49:10 is the principle, *"Unto Him shall the gathering of the people be."* In Psalm 50:5 is the command, *"Gather My saints together unto Me, those that have made a covenant with Me by sacrifice."* Here in Matthew 18:20 is His sweet promise, *"There am I in the midst of them."* The Spirit of God will always gather the saints to God's divine Centre, even to Christ our risen Lord.

> Around Thyself we gladly meet,
> Thine own peculiar treasure,
> And worship in communion sweet,
> with joy that knows no measure.

d. Its authority. "In My Name." Our Lord was about to depart to the Father. The church is called to look after His interests during His absence from earth. Everything the church does in maintaining testimony for God must be regulated by His authority. All that we do must be done in His Name. Divine principles of truth are clearly outlined in the New Testament for the guidance of the collective gatherings of the saints. We do have to adopt methods to carry out these principles, but all methods must maintain the dignity of the truth of God and a reverential behavior in the house of God.

Israel of old had to gather in the place of the Name because, unlike the heathen, their whole devotional life had to be regulated by the Word of God. In the assembly of the Lord the Word of the Lord must be paramount. Before anything new is introduced in any assembly, certain questions should be asked. Is it contrary to divine principles of truth? Will it enhance the glory of God in His own house? Will it maintain the dignity of God's dwelling place? Will it promote unity among the saints or, on the contrary, will it strike a discordant note in the harmony of verse 19?

e. Its beauty — "There am I in the midst." Our blessed Lord who was in the midst of sinners on the cross and is in the midst of the Throne in exaltation today, is now pleased to be in the midst of His gathered people. Each assembly, gathered in subjection to the one Head of the church, is graced by the conscious and precious presence of our adorable Lord.

> He called me out, the Man with garments dyed
> I knew His voice—my Lord, the crucified,
> He showed Himself and Oh, I could not stay,
> I had to follow Him — had to obey.
> It cast me out—this world when once it found
> That I within this rebel heart had crowned
> The Man it had rejected, spurned and slain,
> Whom God in wondrous power had raised
>   to reign;
> And so we are without the camp—my Lord
>   and I,
> But O His presence sweeter is than earthly tie,
> Which once I counted greater than His claim,
> I'm out—not from the world—but to
>   His Name.

6

The Lord's Table and the Lord's Supper

Collectively, the Israelites as a nation were commanded to exercise their religious devotions only *"in the place that the Lord would choose to place His Name."* The reason for this injunction was that their worship (unlike the nations round about them) was to be regulated by the Word of their God. Truth could not share the same place as error, nor could the notions of men share the same authority as the Word of God. Thus we read that the place where God was pleased to place His Name was to be the divine centre of Israel's gatherings (Deut. 12:5). It was the place where they were to bring their gifts and offerings (vs. 6, 7). It was where discipline was to be exercised (17:8-13). It was the place where there was liberty for all God-appointed ministry (18: 6-8). Indeed, it was where the appreciation of the nation could be expressed in what they brought to God (26:1-11).

The New Testament counterpart of this centre is the scriptural assembly of the Lord's people. To this God has linked the authority of His Name, the love of His heart and the wisdom of His mind (Matt. 18:20; 1 Cor. 11:23-26; 5:4; 14:23-26). In 1 Corinthians we are given a picture of the functioning of an assembly that is regulated by the Word of God.

Situated in the very heart of the epistle we have the Lord's table and the Lord's supper. They are brought before us as the expression of a fellowship (10:16-18), the remembrance of a Person (11:23-25), the proclamation of a fact (11:26), and the cherishing of a hope (11:26). This feast of love divine is the centre of the church life of God's people. Any change of emphasis on this fact, or anything that would detract from its importance, is a trend in the wrong direction.

In chapters 10-14 we have a description of the church meeting at which it is celebrated. In these chapters we learn that the Lord's table is linked with the established assembly. It is the centre of all discipline and the place for the exercise of spiritual gift. Both time and spirituality are necessary for such holy exercises. The Lord Himself is in the midst and the physical circle, which the assemblies ought to preserve, is the symbol of that truth.

Let us look at the importance of the Lord's table from the following observations.

1. IN ITS INSTITUTION

(Matt. 26:26-30). In this symbolic act of our Lord we have set forth the great doctrinal truths which are basic and essential to the church's testimony. We read that *"He took bread."* In that act we see the pre-existent Son of God laying hold of perfect humanity. Kinship with the human family was necessary for the redemption of our race. That bread made of fine flour suggests the sinlessness of that humanity. He stood unique among the children of men, unstained by Adam's fall. *"He brake it"* to teach us that the sinless body that He took at incarnation was designed in the counsels of God to be bruised in crucifixion for the sins of the people. He gave it to the disciples and said, *"Take eat, this is My body which is given for you."* In this we learn that His death was substitutionary in character. He took our place, *"the Just for the unjust that He might bring us to God."* In like manner He took the cup and said, *"This is My blood of the new covenant which is shed for many."* In that cup we see the symbol of propitiation or atonement. His death met every claim of divine Justice that was against us. Then He said, *"I will not drink of this fruit of the vine until I drink it new with you in My Father's kingdom."* These triumphant words in the hour of His travail breathe the great truths of His resurrection, ascension and His coming again to reign supreme with His own beloved people,

> O Lord, from Thee the bread we take, from
> Thy pierced hand the wine,
> In rest—accepted for Thy sake—our

meetness, Lord, is Thine.
We praise Thee for this quiet hour, spent
    with Thyself alone,
In which we feel the Spirit's power and all
    His teachings own.

2. IN ITS POSITION

It is the link between the two comings of Christ. It gives the church a look backward to the cross, upward to the throne, and onward to His coming. To quote the words of another, "The Lord's supper is the memorial of a departed Friend, *'This do in remembrance of Me'*; it is the parable of a present Friend, *'For where two or three are gathered together in My Name, There am I in the midst of them'*; it is the prophecy of a returning Friend, *'Till He come.'* " Its celebration therefore is during the night of our Lord's rejection, the only night the church will ever know. Every symbol in the church reminds us of the night. We are compared to stars that shine in the night and to lampstands that Shine in the dark. The supper is an evening meal. But the night is far spent. The darkness will soon be broken by the Bright and Morning Star. Then a new day will dawn when He, as the Sun of righteousness, will rise with healing in His wings.

Earth needs Thee as their King and Jewish
    exiles cry,
"Come, David's Son, to David's throne and
    reign eternally."
The Church amid her tears throughout the
    weary night,
Looks forth to catch the quiv'ring ray of
    morning's dawning
Return, O Lord, return! Why should Thy
    chariot stay?
We long to hear Thy words of love, "Rise up
    and come away."

3. IN ITS NATURE

It calls for the church's purity. It is a moral centre, a test of every conscience. It is in view of the feast that each one is to examine himself before he eats (11:29). It is where the assembly is to act if self-judgement is neglected (ch. 5), and where God acts if the assembly refuses to discharge its responsibility (ch. 11). The Lord's table is before us each time as three types of sins are exposed and rebuked in the Corinthian assembly as a warning to us all. The first concerns the impure sins of the body (ch. 5); the second involves the uncontrollable passions of the soul that disregards the feelings and welfare of fellow saints (ch. 11). The third deals with the sins of the spirit (ch. 10) which involves compromising and fraternizing with the religious world where Christ was dishonoured. In this connection it is well to remember that the lordship of Christ is linked with the assembly in all its functions. We meet on the Lord's day (Rev. 1;10; Acts 20:7), around the Lord's table (1 Cor. 10:16-21), to partake of the Lord's supper (11:20), to proclaim the Lord's death (11:26), to discern the Lord's body (11:29), until the Lord's return (11:26). Oh! for more of a moral and spiritual suitability for the precious presence of our wonderful Lord.

IN ITS APPEAL

The one loaf upon the table is the symbol of the church's unity (10:17). In chapter 10 the bread is the symbol of the mystical body of Christ, whereas in chapter 11 it is the symbol of His literal body. The church is one in spite of the Devil's attacks. It will be preserved in that unity through the prayer of our Lord in John 17 until He comes again. But the only place on earth where a practical expression can be given of that unity is the local assembly of the Lord's people who gather to the one divine Centre in subjection to the risen Head of the church. The Word of God teaches that such is a miniature of the one body, the local expression of the one great whole (12:27).

IN ITS FRUITS

The preservation of assemblies in sound doctrine can be traced to their loyalty in keeping the feast every Lord's day. It is here that we learn afresh the meaning of Calvary. It is in the measure that the Lord's supper has been emphasized that the assemblies have been solidified. Wherever there is a trend away from this emphasis the results are confusion, departure and a craze for something new.

There is nothing sweeter and more assuring than to sit down at the Lord's table, with His own beloved people, to remember Him. What beautiful simplicity to see God's holy priesthood in action as one brother after another leads the assembly in worship! The hymn given out in fellowship with God and the Word of God read at the appropriate time, both contribute to the richness of worship and to the leading of the saints into a deeper appreciation of the person, the sufferings and the glories of our loving Lord. The Spirit leads then to a point at which thanks will be given for the bread and cup. After this the offering will be taken in accordance with 1 Corinthians 16:1, 2, which is an expression of our appreciation of the goodness of God. Then with the whole assembly present and hearts softened by the remembrance of our Lord, there should be time for a brother to rise with a word of edification, exhortation or comfort. We repeat that time and spirituality are required for such a meeting as this. Anything or any activity that would disturb or detract or cut short such a meeting, is an intrusion upon holy ground.

Hush our hearts, as in the sacred Name
We bow in worship and the promise claim —
Where two or three are gathered there am I,
Unseen, yet present to faith's opened eye.

Here in our midst art Thou, O risen Lord,
Worthy, O Lamb once slain, to be adored;
Here in our midst to lead Thy people's praise
And incense sweet unto Thy Father raise.

We do remember Thee as Thou hast said,
And think upon Thee as we break the bread,
Recall Thy dying love, Thy cross and shame,
Drinking the cup of blessing in Thy Name.

Only a little while we pilgrims stay
To spread the table on our desert way,
Soon will He come and coming take us home,
Amen, e'en so, Lord Jesus, quickly come!

7

Reception to God's Assembly

Realizing that we are approaching a most delicate subject, we shall seek to do so with a sincere respect for the consciences of godly saints who may beg to differ with us. Nevertheless, the confusion of thought among the Lord's people today and the growing carelessness toward the rights of God in His own house call for a word of warning to all responsible brethren in the assemblies of the saints.

The guideline for this important subject is not sentimentality, but the Word of God alone. Scripture does not teach that a believer should be received irrespective of moral and doctrinal considerations. Representative brethren at the door of each assembly are there, not only to welcome those who are worthy, but to guard the saints against the unworthy who would take advantage of our Christian liberty (Acts 9:26-28; Jude 4; Rev. 2:2).

Let us recognize clearly that reception in the New Testament is not to the Lord's supper, but into the life of the assembly (Acts 2:42). To extend the privilege of the remembrance feast to those who have no convictions as to the truth of the assembly tends to mar the order of God and leaves the assembly exposed to many dangers. It makes the assembly the stamping ground of every religious wanderer and the target for the spread of error. History has shown that when an assembly substitutes convenience for conviction and godly order it leads to the disruption of the simple testimony of God.

When truth is bought at a price, it is loved and appreciated. But when the assembly is made a mere convenience for the fickle and the unexercised, it cheapens the precious things of God. Such people never add stability to God's testimony. When the disciples watched the Lamb of God as He walked (John 1), they cried, *"Where dwellest Thou?"* Our Lord's reply was, *"Come and see."* The dwelling place of Christ in the midst of His own is reached by spiritual exercise. The pearls of truth are not to be handed out to the careless to be used and abused. Moreover, the Lord's dwelling place was a nameless place. What a rebuke to the Babel of tongues and names in Christendom today. From that centre they went out to serve and to that centre they brought the converts.

We shall now look to the Word of God. "To the Word and to the Testimony" is always the safest guide. The epistle to the Romans is foundational. In this letter, the first of the seven church epistles, we may expect some instruction on this important subject. In reading this epistle carefully we learn that there are three aspects of reception mentioned.

1. THE RECEPTION OF THE YOUNG CONVERT

"Him that is weak in the faith, receive you" (14:1). This is the picture of the young convert just coming out of Judaism with some of the graveclothes still clinging to him. For him the assembly will be a nursery. The word "receive" here means to take to yourselves in kindness. They were not to judge his doubtful thoughts (Marg., A.V.). As the young believer grows in the things of God his scruples will soon disappear. We may assume that he was already baptized. The order of this foundational epistle would clearly indicate that baptism had already taken place with all the saints. In chapters four and five we have obedience linked with salvation, resulting in life being imparted. In chapter six obedience is linked with baptism, resulting in life being manifested as seen in chapters seven and eight. Then in chapter fourteen obedience is linked with reception and behavior in the local assemblies of the Lord's people. The assemblies seldom have any trouble with the young convert who shows signs of divine life in the soul. When he is baptized and seeks the fellowship of the local assembly, the elder brethren know that he is in the impressionable stage. As he learns the ways of God and the Word of God in fellowship with the Lord's people,

the old graveclothes will soon fall off and he will walk, work and worship in the liberty of the sons of God.

2. RECEPTION FROM NEIGHBOURING ASSEMBLIES

"Wherefore receive ye one another, as Christ also received us, to the glory of God" (15:7). No verse has been more abused than this one. It has been used to throw the door of the assembly wide open to everyone who says he is a Christian. Someone has said that a text taken out of its context only becomes a pretext. If we look at the context of the last three chapters of Romans we will discover that there were at least three assemblies in the city of Rome (16:5, 14, 15). Paul was writing to those saints who were already in assembly fellowship. But with Jewish and Gentile prejudices they were tempted to raise barriers against each other. Hence the exhortation for each assembly to receive from the other. Their differences were not fundamental. Meats and holy days did not affect moral or doctrinal soundness. To bring into harmony two classes, as Jew and Gentile, with their two different cultures and backgrounds, Paul by the Spirit lays down four simple guidelines.

First, the liberty of the individual conscience (14:5), *"Let every man be fully persuaded in his own mind."* The conscience, of course, must be enlightened and guided by truth alone. When one is not condemned by either precept or practice, he must act before the Lord alone. Christ must never be displaced as Lord in the realm of the individual conscience.

In the light of this principle there is pressed upon the saints four simple considerations.

a. There will always be a variety of grades in Christian attainment. We read of the weak and the strong and there will always be the babes, the young men and the fathers. Paul in another epistle puts it like this, *"Nevertheless, whereunto we have already attained, let us walk by the same rule"* (Phil. 3:16). I must not make my attainment the measure and rule for my brethren.

b. Though we are joined in the fellowship of the local assembly, each believer retains his own individuality (v. 4), *"Who art thou that judgest another man's servant? To his own Master he standest or fallest. Yea, he shall be holden up: for God is able to make him stand."* Christian honesty before the Lord is the path that leads to harmonious Christian fellowship in the assembly.

c. Devotion to the Lord alone is the secret of true holiness (vs. 7-9), *"Whether we live, we live unto the Lord . . . for to this end Christ both died and rose and revived that He might be Lord."* He who loves the Lord and lives only for His glory, will grow in the graces of the Master.

d. The Lord alone is the true Monarch of the soul (v. 6), *"He that eateth, eateth unto the Lord."*

Second, there will be accountability to the Lord alone (vs. 10-12), *"We shall all stand before the judgement seat of Christ... so then every one of us shall give account of himself to God."* Though not accountable to our brethren in our growth in holiness, we will be to the Lord. Oh! to be acceptable to our Lord in that day (2 Cor. 5:9).

Third, we must regard the feelings of others (v. 13), *"But judge this rather, that no man put a stumblingblock or an occasion to fall in his brother's way."* We must seek to maintain the delicate balance of living for the glory of God and the welfare of His people. I must not be offensive to my brethren or stumble a weak believer.

Fourth, all actions must be the fruit of an endeavor to please God, *"Whatsoever is not of faith is sin"* (v. 23). These principles relative to individual behavior are applicable to assemblies in their behavior to each other as our context shows. There is a fellowship of assemblies, but each is responsible not to do or adopt anything that would be offensive to other assemblies and thus mar the endeavor to keep the unity of the Spirit in the bond of peace.

3. THE RECEPTION OF THE VISITOR WHO TRAVELS TO DISTANT POINTS

"I commend unto you Phebe our sister, who is a servant of the church which is at Cenchrea, that ye receive her in the Lord, as becometh saints." (16:1, 2). Phebe was going to a place where she was unknown. She carried a letter of commendation which bore

witness to her character and standing in the church at Cenchrea. Such a practice would be superfluous if, as some say, we are to receive the stranger on his own testimony. If the early saints saw the value of letters of commendation why, in a time when there is more profession and error than ever before, do some want to ignore them? Elder brethren have a responsibility to see that a letter is given to one of their number who is going to another assembly where he is not known, and the other assembly has a right to look for one.

We must always remember that each church epistle was written to a recognized fellowship of saints with their bishops and deacons (Phil. 1:1). One of these churches was reminded that there is *"a within and without"* with a responsibility to judge them that are within (1 Cor. 5). May we ask how the right of discipline could be exercised except upon those who are part of the local assembly?

While it is true that all saints in any locality constitute a witness for God in that place (and for this we give God thanks), it is also true that each New Testament assembly had a recognized fellowship, meeting in one place (1 Cor. 11:20), each with its own government or oversight to guide the saints and to exercise discipline whenever required.

The simple New Testament order cannot be improved upon, or added to. It is summed up in Acts two as Conviction, Conversion, Confession — they were baptized, Continuance — they continued in the apostles' doctrine, in fellowship, in the breaking of bread and prayers, Consecration — they placed their all on the altar for God.

At the risk of getting into issues that are more delicate and complicated, I would like to say a word on the reception of distinguished gifts that the risen Head has given to the church (Eph. 4:11). Here too there must be honest and scriptural discrimination. In days of declension, carelessness and the lack of spiritual discernment on the part of so-called elders, letters of commendation have been handed out indiscriminately. These are intended to commend workers to full-time service for the Lord. Some use these to travel from assembly to assembly with little or no ministry for the Lord's people and no desire to pioneer with the Gospel. The sad result is that at home and on the mission field so many misfits have crowded into the work of the Lord, creating no end of difficulties and headaches for the saints. Others with no convictions as to assembly principles will spend much of their time visiting in the denominations of men, helping to build up that which is not of God. With an increasing trend toward interdenominationalism, many of God's people have been thrown into confusion; like silly doves have lost all sense of spiritual direction. When the line of demarcation between the assemblies and the religious world of man is broken down, the ways of the religious world are copied and introduced to the assemblies. To be specific, because of the prosperity of some fundamental denominations under one-man ministry, some among the assemblies feel we should educate certain young men to be pastors of (not "in") assemblies. It is the same spirit of laziness on the part of responsible brethren that created clericalism in the early days of the church. It is a willingness on the part of some to pay a man to do their work for them.

Parallel with an increase of worldliness among us and a lack of the sense of the power of God, there is an increase in the activities of the flesh. New movements have arisen in professedly assembly circles which are, to say the least, decidedly contrary to New Testament principles. Young people are pressed to go abroad for Christian work. Many have responded who never learned to do Christian work in their own home community. The spirit of religious adventure has become most popular. Yet because it has a missionary emphasis it has gained widespread support. A group of leaders in a certain place tell the young people where to go, how long they have to stay and where they have to go next when their time is up. Beloved, this is not the pattern of the New Testament. The prerogatives of the divine Spirit are not to be usurped by men. We do not doubt the godliness and zeal of many of these dear young people. We simply point out that they are being led in ways that are contrary to the path of the Spirit in the Acts of the apostles (see 16: 6-10) .

It is because of this declension from assembly principles that elder brethren are responsible to guard the saints from the inroads of anything that would negate the truths for which assemblies have always stood. No assembly is under any obligation to recognize any professed servant of Christ who is not doing the work of God in God's way or building up the saints in the right ways of the Lord.

On the other hand we must beware of another extreme attitude that would refuse honoured servants of Christ for no other reason than that they visited other assemblies of which certain leaders disapprove. I refer to men who are assembly men, men whose ministry and character are known among the saints, men whose lives have been lived for God and the assemblies of His people. These men are too well taught in the word of truth to believe in a confederacy of assemblies, whether on the right hand or the left. They are too honest to be bought. They are too loyal to their Lord to be moved from the path of faithfulness, either by money or persecution. They judge each assembly as they find it and wherever there is room for the whole Word of God and liberty to minister it, they will seek to help the saints and encourage them in the right ways of the Lord. Yet such gifts from the risen Head of the church have been refused in certain circles, and that for no other reason than that they refuse to recognize confederacy. Thus the saints in these assemblies have been deprived of their rich ministry, a ministry designed of the Spirit of God for their edification.

To overstep the Word of God in ecclesiastical procedure will only lead to confusion and bitterness. To try to make Scripture mean what it does not mean in order to bolster partisan cause among the Lord's people is dangerous business indeed. How many godly servants of Christ, yea, how many godly saints have had meted out to them that which is for "wicked persons"? So many who have professed to be most zealous for the truth have been loveless men. They have proved on occasions to be conscienceless, too, in ostracizing many of the choicest saints of God. It is to be observed in Third John that the man who loved to put the godly out of the church was the man who *"loved to have the pre-eminence."* Was such marked by *"love to all the saints"*? Nay, his love for place left no room for love to God or love to the people of God. Godly Gaius, Demetrius and John all suffered from his hand. Gaius still held fast to the truth and walked in

61

it. He received the stranger and was commended for it. Godly Demetrius went forth *"for His Name's sake, taking nothing of the Gentiles."* To receive such was obligatory. John said to Gaius, *"Beloved, do not imitate what is evil but what is good."* The evil was the refusing, and the good was the receiving of such brethren.

I am sure that God is speaking to many of the assemblies of His people. We must have an ear to hear what the Spirit saith unto the churches. Beloved, let our measuring line be that of the Sanctuary in our judgement of God's dear people. Let us not lightly set aside men whose character and ministry are unquestionable and whose lives are dedicated to the building up of the assemblies of God's people. Every godly servant of Christ must at all cost maintain his liberty to move in the current of the will of God. He will seek with much longsuffering to build according to the divine pattern and establish the saints in truth and love. Such men will only do the assemblies good. The assemblies who receive them will receive the blessing of God. Those who refuse them must bear that responsibility before the Lord.

Is this appeal uncalled for? Have we not seen such men rejected, their godly lives and rich ministry regarded as worthless, solely upon the ground of what assemblies they have visited? Have we not seen others with less character and little ministry received and acknowledged because they sought to please certain factional men? To create an atmosphere that becomes a haven for men of disputatious spirits, regardless of character, men must act independently of the Spirit of God. When the predominance of our zeal is turned to the building up of a party among the assemblies of the saints, we can be sure that the formation of the life of Jesus will be stayed in the soul. It will narrow our vision, dry up the springs of our affections and wither those virtues of "the new man" so that our love cannot flow out to all the saints impartially. It will lead to the loss of all that spiritual ability to keep a proper brotherly attitude to all saints and yet to remain separate from evil principles that engulf many of them. Let us never forget that the Devil's victories among us are a reproach to us all. Shall we never learn that discord among the assemblies is not only a triumph for the Devil, a dishonour to the holy Name of our Lord whom we love and wish to please, but also the cause of all our barrenness and impoverishment? My beloved brethren, I appeal for godly humility. I ask a return to first love, first works and first principles. God's order of reception is clear. If we follow it we will be saved from extremes and be protected from error.

> Life is too brief between the budding and the
> falling leaf,
> Between the seed time and the golden sheaf,
> for hate and spite.
> We have no time for malice and for greed,
> therefore with love
> Make beautiful the deed, fast speeds the night.

8

The Church and the Churches

One of the first questions that confronts the young convert is, "What church shall I join?" If he looks at Christendom with its variety of denominations and sects, he will receive baffling answers. "To the Word and to the Testimony" is always the safest guide for the path of faith.

As the young believer reads his Bible, he will learn that there is only one true Church. It is built upon the Rock, Christ Jesus (Matt. 16) and composed of all believers who are purchased by the Blood of the Lamb (Acts 20:28). This one and only Church is compared to a Body, possessed with the life and nature of God (Eph. 1); it is likened to a Temple or Building, possessed with the presence of the Holy Spirit (Eph. 2); it is viewed as a Bride, filled with the love of the Heavenly Bridegroom (Eph. 5). The seven bonds that bind all in this bundle of life are one Body, one Spirit, one Hope, one Lord, one Faith, one Baptism, one God and Father of all (Eph. 4:4-7). What a consolation to know that every child of God, at his conversion, has been baptized in one Spirit into the Body of Christ (1 Cor. 12:13)! Our sins are gone, and life, peace and hope have become the foretaste of better things to come. This is the Church for which *"Christ gave Himself"* (Eph. 5:25), whose invisible unity is preserved by the Spirit of God, in fulfilment of our Lord's prayer in John 17. That Church will rise to meet her Lord in the air at His coming. It is God's Ambassador of peace to the nations, preaching peace by Jesus Christ. She is the Repository and Guardian of God's truth on earth (1 Tim. 3:15), the salt of the earth and the light of the world.

Christ is her foundation
Humility is her dress
Unity is her ideal
Reconciliation is her message
Charity is her bond
Heaven is her destiny.

The young believer will also learn from the Word of God that there is a local expression of the one true Church in the company of God's people, meeting together in their own locality in humble subjection to the risen Head of the Church. Thus we read of "the church of God which is at Corinth" (1 Cor. 1:1, 2). All the believers at Corinth met in one place (11:20), but if the number became too large for one building, there would be a hive-off. When the Gospel spread and new companies of believers were formed to gather in the Name of our Lord alone, the plural was used and we read of "the churches of the saints."

Let me differentiate between two expressions in the New Testament relative to the local assembly: the one is "of the church" (Acts 8:1-4) and the other "in the church" (1 Cor. 11:18). The first means that representatively each member of the local assembly is part of that assembly twenty-four hours a day, no matter where he or she may be. In our behaviour we are going to either enhance its testimony or bring reproach upon it. The second refers to our coming together in assembly capacity when we meet in one place.

Each local assembly becomes a miniature of the whole. It is the responsibility of every child of God to identify himself with the local assembly of the Lord's people and share the privileges and responsibilities of God's testimony in that locality.

The question may be asked, "How is the New Testament church to be distinguished from man's religious systems around us?" The answer is, only as it expresses the truth of the whole and functions according to the principles of the whole. Let us look at some distinguishing marks of the New Testament church as seen in 1 Corinthians:

The queen of Sheba came to see the wisdom of Solomon. In 1 Corinthians we see the glory of a greater than Solomon. She came with all her hard questions. She had problems beyond the wisest of her counsellors, but not beyond the wisdom of Israel's king. In 1 Corinthians 1 we see the wisdom of a greater than Solomon. He is God's answer for all our needs. For our moral and spiritual needs, God has made Christ unto us wisdom, righteousness, sanctification and redemption (v. 30). In these four great words we see Christ as the answer to the degradation of sin, the debt of sin, the defilement of sin and the dominion of sin. For our ecclesiastical needs God has made the Name of Christ the one unifying force for His people (v. 10). Each New Testament church refuses all denominational tags. 1 Corinthians 1 teaches us a divine principle that will guide us in the midst of religious confusion. Any name or names that we may assume that do not embrace the whole are sectarian. Paul rebukes the Corinthians for their factionalism in saying, "I am of Paul, and I am of Aponos, and I of Cephas, and I of Christ." Each name embraced only each party to the exclusion of all other believers. The Spirit of God then points to three serious sins that are committed in assuming sectarian names. It is a sin against the Person of Christ — "Is Christ divided?" It is a sin against the work of Christ — "Was Paul crucified for you?" It is a sin against the Name of Christ — "Were you baptized in the name of Paul?" (vv. 12, 13). The one name of our beloved Lord is set over against all other names as the only Name that can unite the saints in a practical way (v. 10). The truth of gathering in His Name alone, means to gather in subjection to the authority of Christ which is enshrined in His lovely Name.

The queen's attention was drawn to the house that Solomon had built. This is the subject of chapter 3. The local church, like the whole, is a temple of God, built upon Christ the Rock and composed of living stones. Israel built for Pharoah storehouses of wood, hay and stubble. Solomon built for God a temple of gold, silver and precious stones (v. 10). The living stones of God's temple, the Church, take on their adornment when they take on the character of God. They are to shine with a beauty not their own.

She saw the meat of his table. But behold the feast of a greater than Solomon in chapter 5, *"Let us keep the feast . . . with the unleavened bread of sincerity and truth."* What bountiful provision God has prepared for His own.

She saw the sitting of his servants and their apparel. This is the subject Paul discusses in chapter 11. There we behold the saints gathered for the weekly celebration of the Lord's supper. Their deportment is specially mentioned as teaching angels the manifold wisdom of God. In a world where men dress like women and women like men, it is well for the saints of God to maintain these God-given distinguishing marks between male and female, both in dress and place as demanded in the order of God.

The queen also beheld the attendance of his ministers and his cupbearers. This is the subject of chapters 12-14. In these we see a variety of gift to meet a variety of need. There is a divine liberty for every joint to supply that which is necessary for the health and growth of the whole.

Then she saw the ascent by which Solomon went up to the house of the Lord. This is the truth of chapter 15. There we see the ascent of a greater than Solomon to the right hand of God. In His resurrection and ascension the saints are assured of a grand immortality.

Let us look at 1 Corinthians 10-14 in a little more detail. In chapter 10 we are taught moral suitability for God's assembly. The failure of Israel and their subsequent chastisement are held up as a warning to us all that holiness and sin cannot walk together. Indicated in the five "alls" in verses 1-4 are five blessings by which Israel was enriched of God. The cloud pointed to their protection and the Red Sea to their justification. They were baptized unto a new leadership as they said farewell to the bondage of Egypt. They fed on angel's food and drank the water from the smitten rock. But they rebelled and became dissatisfied with God's food (v. 6 and Numbers 11:4-6), with the true worship of God (v. 7 and Exodus 32: 6), with God's separation (v. 8 and Numbers 25:1-9), with God's path and leading (v. 9 and Numbers 21:4), with God's chastisement (v. 10 and Numbers 16:41-50). Thus their spiritual declension began with their thought life (v. 6). It spread to affect their spiritual life (v. 7), their social life (v. 8), their individual life (v. 9) and their congregational life (v. 10).

For our protection, lest we like Israel, lose moral suitability for the testimony of God on earth. Paul points to three safeguards: the first is, know thyself (v. 12), *"Wherefore let him that thinketh he standeth take heed lest he fall"* A consciousness of our weakness will lead us to lean hard on the Arm of Almighty Strength. The second is, know thy God (v. 13), *"There hath no temptation taken you but such as is common to man; but God is faithful who will not suffer you to be tempted above that ye are able; but will with the temptation also make a way to escape that ye may be able to bear it."* The third is, know the deceitfulness of sin (v. 14), *"Wherefore, my dearly beloved, flee from idolatry."* The first will preserve our thought life, the second our spiritual life and the third our congregational life.

This is followed by a picture of three tables, symbols of three fellowships. A Jew's presence at the altar or table of Judaism indicated his identification with that system of which the table was the expression. A pagan's presence at the table of demons meant his identification with that system of which the table was the expression. In contrast to both we have the Lord's table. A believer's presence there is indicative of his identification with Christ and his fellowship with the Father and the Son. The cup comes first (v. 16) because the blood of atonement has bought us out of Judaism and paganism and has introduced us to a new fellowship, the fellowship of the body of Christ symbolized by the one bread (v. 17). The Lord's table therefore in chapter 10, is an appeal for our separation, morally and religiously, that we might be suitable to God and instruments of divine purpose.

It may be observed that a Jew was a partaker of the altar (v. 18) during the sacrifice of the peace-offering. This is the aspect of the Cross that is seen in the Lord's supper as we meet to remember Him.

In chapter 11 we have deportment that becometh the house of God. When we come together in church, the male uncovers his head. Since Christ is the Head of every man this teaches us that He, Christ our Head, must never be covered. The aim of the Spirit of God in the assembly is to unveil Christ, in all His glory, to every eye.

The female covers her head because, *"the head of every woman is the man."* By covering her head she, symbolically, puts man, her head, out of sight. The glory of God must displace the glory of man. Every intrusion of the flesh in the assembly is rebuked by the covered heads of the sisters. How careful then we should be that every devotional act in public assembly is the result of deep exercise before the Lord and in response to the divine guidance of the Spirit of God.

> O may we in Thy love abide
> And with Thy truth be satisfied
>> And all Thy grace explore.
> Teach us Thy lowly mind
> And in Thyself alone to find
>> Our fulness more and more.

9

Gifts, Principles and Responsibilities
1 Corinthians 12

In going through 1 Corinthians 12-14 we are impressed by the fact that the assembly is the place for the exercise of spiritual gift, not for the exhibition of natural talent. Two things are most prominent in these chapters, the divine Sovereignty of the Holy Spirit to impart gift to be used for His glory and the divine Liberty to exercise gift as He would lead. The purpose in the exercise of gift is twofold: to exalt Christ as Lord and to build up the saints in the ways of God (12:3, 7).

Verse one begins with, *"Now concerning spiritualities, brethren, I would not have you to be ignorant."* In the previous chapters the writer had been dealing with carnalities. These were divisions in the assembly (ch. 1-4), sensuality in individuals (ch. 5-7) and undue license in social and church relationships (ch. 8-11).

The section of the epistle we are now considering (ch. 12- 14) presents a corrective ministry from the Spirit of God which, if accepted, would result in the proper adjustment of these evils. In the twelfth chapter, the unity of the body of Christ is a rebuke to the spirit of schism in the church. According to chapter thirteen, the purity of the love of Christ exposes the depravity of sensuality. The fourteenth chapter deals with Christian liberty in contrast to fleshly license. Let us now look at

THE UNITY OF THE BODY

The unity of the Godhead, of Father, Son and Holy Spirit, is set forth in verses 1-11; whereas the unity of the mystical Body of Christ, the result of divine affinity which binds one member to another, appears in verses 12-31. Unity expressed in this two-fold manner, is mentioned by Christ in His high-priestly prayer in John 17, and by Paul, through the Spirit, in his Ephesian letter (4:4-7). Thus when the church functions according to the mind of the divine Spirit, there will be a manifestation given, both of the unity of the Godhead and the unity of the Body. The unity of the Godhead is from eternity, that of the church since Pentecost. The unity of the Godhead is fully revealed in heaven, that of the Body of Christ ought to be expressed on earth.

The ultimate source of all spiritual gift lies within the Godhead (vv. 4-6), in the same Spirit, the same Lord (Jesus) and in the same God (the Father). Every gift imparted to man by God, has as its final objective the acknowledging of Christ as Lord (v. 3). At the same time, in a secondary way, the solemn duty of each gift is the profit and common welfare of every believer (v. 7).

The heavenly endowments referred to in verses 4-6 provide the equipment by which the church edifies herself in love, and by which she proclaims the Gospel entrusted to her. In these verses mention is made of *"gifts," "administrations"* and *"operations."* These may be defined thus: gifts in their variety, are the divinely imparted capabilities for service; administrations refer to the opportunities God gives for His service; operations would suggest the different methods by which we go about our service. God in His wisdom fits men by personality, ability and the grace of His Spirit to perform the specific work He has assigned to each member of the Body of Christ.

There are nine spiritual gifts contemplated in verses 8-10. These are arranged in groups of three. The first group has wisdom, knowledge and faith, and has to do with the revelation of the truth. It is significant that wisdom comes first. The proverb says, *"Wisdom is the principal thing; therefore get wisdom."* Wisdom is the art of right acting as knowledge is the art of right thinking. Faith is absolute confidence in the truth that is revealed. There may be a suggestion here that the gift of the pastor is specially linked with *"wisdom,"* that of the teacher with *"knowledge"* and that of the evangelist with *"faith."*

The second group deals with the spectacular display of God's power in *"healings," "miracles" and "prophecies."* Power that is delegated to the church is done so through the Holy Spirit. Such power may change its means of manifestation according to the necessity in the purpose of God. This we shall see in chapter 13.

The third group has *"the discerning of spirits," "diverse kinds of tongues"* and *"the interpretation of tongues,"* and has to do with the spiritual ability to discern both truth and error, and to differentiate between the work of the Spirit and the activity of the flesh. This is referred to as *"the smelling"* in verse 17.

PRINCIPLES OF UNITY

There are four purposeful principles to control the relationships of our congregational lives. When these are fully acknowledged there will be a clear expression of the unity of the Body of Christ.

1. The sense of responsibility devolving upon each gifted saint to function within the sphere that corresponds to his gift (vv. 15, 16), *"If the foot shall say, Because I am not the hand, I am not of the body, is it therefore not of the body?"* The acceptance of this responsibility is a protection against negligence, and places upon all a particular ministry to discover and to perform. It will deliver from spiritual laziness.

2. There is a blessed variety existing within the unity which characterizes the church of God. This presents the second principle. We read, *"If the whole body were an eye, where were the hearing?" "Now are they many members,* (foot, hand or eye) *yet but one body"* (vv. 17-20, 28-30). There is no gift that performs every function essential to the well-being of the whole, but every function is executed by the combined action of every separate gift operating within its own sphere. The understanding of this principle produces a rebuke to the spirit of jealousy and destroys the monotony of a one-man ministry.

3. The third principle reveals the necessity for all. The organic oneness of the Body of Christ is such that there is an interdependence among all the several members. Such is the divine

cohesion that each member functions within its own sphere, nevertheless, all the several functions are perfectly coordinated (vv. 21-25), *"And the eye cannot say unto the hand, I have no need of thee."* In government each local church stands independent the one from the other, wholly responsible to the Lord (Rev. 2, 3). In the fellowship of the Body the saints are so interdependent that independency finally results in poverty of soul. When one member says to another, "I have no need of thee," a schism is formed in the Body and the harmony of its function is marred.

The local assemblies of the Lord's people have a priceless heritage to guard. To meet in the Name of our Lord Jesus Christ alone where these divine principles have liberty to function is indeed an honour and a privilege. Let us beware lest worldly innovations, human cleverness and man's ability to organize, do not displace what is divine and of God with that which is human and of man.

4. The last of these principles describes the union of all the members. It is such an organic union that what affects one member affects all. For this reason each member is called upon to contribute to the spiritual health and welfare of the whole. This would embrace acts of sympathy and selflessness for, if *"one member suffer, all the members suffer with it; or one member be honoured, all the members rejoice with it"* (v. 26). Suspicion affects the spirit of the assembly, destroying that mutual peace and joy which springs from the presence of mutual confidence. Oh, for a larger heart to feel the sorrows of the saints and to share their joys. Mutual respect promotes spiritual unity and helps to make us strong for our work and witness among men.

For those who think they have no gift with which to serve the Lord there is a word of encouragement in verse 28. It is the little word *"helps."* The corresponding verb is found in Acts 20:35, 1 Timothy 6:2 and Luke 1:54. From its usage we may suggest that the succoring of the weak, the tending of the sick and helping of the needy is part of the functions of the Body, for which there should be an exercise to engage in for the glory of God.

If these divine principles are recognized and obeyed, the evils (which may be compared to flies in the ointment of the apothecary) of spiritual laziness, of monotony, of independency and suspicion will be banished and a sweeter reflection of the character of the Lord Jesus will enrich our testimony on earth.

> So weak, so frail an instrument, if Thou,
>   my God, vouchsafe to use,
> 'Tis praise enough to be employed, reward
>   enough, if Thou excuse.
> If Thou excuse, then work Thy will by so unfit
>   an instrument;
> It will at once Thy goodness show and prove
>   Thy power omnipotent.

10

The More Excellent Way
1 Corinthians 13

The heart of I Corinthians is chapter thirteen. It is here that the variety of gift in chapter twelve is baptized in the sea of love and rises in chapter fourteen to function under the control of the Spirit of God. In chapter twelve we have the sphere of ministry, here in chapter thirteen we have the spirit of ministry. Moreover, the impurity that is born of carnality (ch. 5-7) is not seen here, for there is no impurity in love.

The apostle, moved by the Spirit of inspiration, gives us the most wonderful treatise on love in the New Testament, maintaining that it is the greatest virtue in Christian character. In this treatise we see the Superiority of love (vv. 1-3), the Sweetness of love (vv. 4-7) and the Stability of love (vv. 8-13) .

THE SUPERIORITY OF LOVE

The three constituent parts of man's personality are ever active, the heart (v. 1), the mind (v. 2) and the will (v. 3). But every emotion of our being receives its importance and value only when love is supreme. In the work of evangelism the sweet sound of the Gospel loses its harmony and song when love is lacking (v. 1); love is greater than eloquence. *"Sounding brass and tinkling cymbal"* is simply noise without tune. Love displaces discord with harmony and enables our lives to take on a song.

In the realm of teaching, love alone gives effectiveness to all our ability (v. 2). Divine love in operation is greater than the gift of prophecy or the understanding of mysteries; greater than knowledge and greater than faith. Though we may have all these endowments their use will yield no profit if love is missing.

In the discharge of pastoral duties or of shepherd care, love gives meaning to all self-denial (v. 3). Such sacrificial service loses its whole value if love is wanting, for love is greater than sacrifice and greater than charity.

Of what worth are the most flowery sermons, the greatest achievements in gift or talent, or the most self-denying efforts in the service of God, if deficient in love? The spirit that gives value to all ministry is missing, leaving us with formality that is dead, even though it may be correct. It is only when love controls the heart, the mind and the will, that we rise to the norm of true Christian living.

The Thessalonians, in the beauty of first love, were characterized by their work of faith, their labour of love and their patience of hope. In contrast we have the Ephesians whose heart had grown cold. They had works and toil and patience, but faith, hope and love were missing. Our Lord warned that there either must be recovery or the lampstand would be removed, for a testimony without love is an insult to heaven and a misrepresentation of God to men.

> Long we have our burden borne, our own
> unfaithfulness,
> Object of the heathen's scorn, who mocks our
> scanty grace.
> Jesus, our reproach remove, let sin no more
> Thy people shame,
> Show us rooted in Thy love, in life and death
> the same.

THE SWEETNESS OF LOVE

Like Ezekiel's river, the love of Christ sweetens and heals wherever it flows. If love is indispensable in verses 1-3, it is invaluable in verses 4-7. *"Love suffereth long and is kind."* It does not act impatiently towards those whose failures grieve us.

"Love envieth not." It does not repine over another's success. *"Love vaunteth not itself."* It does not parade its own importance as did the Pharisees. *"Is not puffed up."* Four times over in chapters 4 and 5 Paul warns of this danger. Where there is a puffing up there is no building up. *"It doth not behave itseif unseemly."* True Christian refinement will always reflect the graces of the Master. He was ever polite, courteous and gentlemanly. *"Love is not easily provoked."*

It does not allow itself to become incensed over un-Christ-like behaviour of others. *"Thinketh no evil."* It does not keep an account of other's failures nor gloat over the weaknesses of the saints, for *"it rejoiceth not in iniquity but rejoiceth in the truth."* It finds true joy when the Lord's people are walking in faith, hope and love. *"It beareth all things, believeth all things, hopeth all things, endureth all things."* It throws a covering over the failures of the saints when there is no scriptural reason to expose them. It is without that deadly spirit of suspicion which is so destructive of Christian fellowship. It hopes for the best in God's people and endures many disappointments in the waiting. *"Love never faileth."* It stands by the saints to the end and endures to the uttermost. The power of God may be witnessed in the exercise of spiritual gift. His very nature is seen in love.

> Thou wouldst like sinful man be made in
>   everything but sin,
> That we as like Thee might become as we
>   unlike have been.
> Like Thee in faith, in meekness, love, in every
>   heavenly grace,
> More of Thine image daily gain till we behold
>   Thy face.

THE STABILITY OF LOVE

The apostle now draws a contrast (vv. 8-13), not between heaven and earth, but between what was to be temporary in the church and what was to be the norm of church life during the dispensation of her pilgrimage. Prophecies, tongues and knowledge (direct communications from God by special revelation) were to fail, halt or vanish away. This was to take place when the perfect thing would come (v. 10). The perfect thing is the completed New Testament (Col. 1:25), the totality of truth as God meant to reveal it. Without this completed thing, he says, "our knowledge is fragmentary, but when the total ensues, the fragmentary becomes antiquated" (Virkuyl trans.). The writer now gives us two illustrations of the position of God's people in the absence of the completed Word of God. The first is the picture of immaturity (v. 11), *"When I was a child I spake as a child ... but when I became a man I put away childish things."* The miraculous gifts of the early church were designed of God in the absence of the completed revelation of truth and to lead it from childhood to maturity.

The second is the picture of imperception (v. 12), *"Now we see through a glass, darkly; but then face to face."* The mirror of truth in the Old Testament was blurred. It was hidden in type and shadow. It needed the revelation of the New Testament to make it clear. Truth then would be divinely harmonized and understood. Until the total ensued the saints could only know in part. In this connection we may think of Moses who saw God face to face at the giving of the law (Num. 14:14). But now we see God face to face through a clearer glass. The Spirit here impresses upon us the thought that though the external helps in the service of the church would be withdrawn, its service and testimony would remain unmarred. The internal virtues of character, would abide. The ministry of the church therefore is not a ministry of the spectacular but of character — faith, hope and love abide. God's power is now manifested in the transformed lives of His own beloved people.

In the service of the church, teaching takes the place of prophecy (compare v. 8 with 2 Pet. 2:1), the worldwide witness of the church takes the place of the gift of tongues. That gift was a sign to the Jewish nation that it had failed to share the knowledge of God with men of other tongues and that God, on its rejection, would choose another vessel, the church, to carry the Gospel to men of all languages (14:1). The special gift of knowledge is displaced by the revelation of God's mind, permanently enshrined in the written Word and discerned by the spiritual in every generation.

Any modern claim to a revival of the gift of tongues or special revelations, apart from the Word of God, is a deception of Satan by which he leads astray simple souls with psychic experiences which are spurious and false.

Here is the more excellent way, the true spirit of Christian testimony. Let the river of His love flow into our hearts in all its fulness. It will enrich our lives, sweeten our disposition and give value to all that we do for Christ. Let us follow after love for it is the crowning virtue of Christian character. It is indispensable (vv. 1-3), invaluable in our service (vv. 4-7) and infallible in our adjustments with the saints of God (vv. 8-13). If, like Ephesus, we leave it, we will be as Samson, when he lost the crown of his Nazariteship, we will go out as at other times and wist not that the Lord has departed from us in all His power and beauty.

The love of our blessed Redeemer claims our affections (Eph. 3:14), it should control our activities (2 Cor. 5:14), and assures our victory (Rom. 8:35). Here is the love of Christ for the student, the servant and the soldier. Faith unites us to Christ and secures for us the forgiveness of sins and life everlasting. Hope brightens the present with the assurance of a triumphant future. Love turns the wilderness of our lives into the garden of the Lord. In all things set love upon the throne, "fair, luminous and pure," to bless and gladden our lives, our homes and our assemblies.

> Great yearning love, no human lips may tell it,
> A love more deep than human heart may
>   know,
> A love that stooped from heaven's highest glory
> To taste of death, its bitterness and woe.
>
> Such is the love that lusters every sorrow,
> A love that makes my cup of joy run o'er;
> That wise, strong love I'll trust with each
>   tomorrow
> Until I tread the desert path no more.

11

Spirit Controlled Ministry
1 Corinthians 14

Paul, in chapters 8-11, reveals the encroachments of carnality in the church life of the saints at Corinth. Here in chapter 14 he administers a specific rebuke to the evident license given to the flesh. True Christian liberty is seen in the control of the Spirit of God in all the exercises of the saints. In this one chapter there are at least seven divine principles which constitute the claims of the lordship of Christ over His own house. The influence of the Holy Spirit is seen to be, not only the power of ministry, but the restraint of ministry as well. The authority of the Lord over His own is indicated by that little word *"let"* used more than a dozen times in the chapter. Let us now look at this godly order in the assembly of the saints.

1. THE QUALITY OF MINISTRY

All oral ministry must be to edification, exhortation and comfort (v. 3). Edification is for the mind, exhortation for the conscience and comfort for the heart. The first builds up the church in the art of right thinking, the second stirs up the church in the art of right acting and the third binds up the wounds of the discouraged and broken-hearted and restores right feeling. Holy Ghost ministry will thus have variety to meet the variety of need among the people of God.

2. THE COMMUNICATION OF MINISTRY

All ministry must be intelligible to the listeners (v. 9), *"Except ye utter by the tongue words easy to be understood, how shall it be known what is spoken?"* The glory of God and the welfare of the saints must ever be before the speaker. The minister of the Word of God must speak from clarity of thought, with plainness of speech and from heart to heart, if divine truths are to be understood by the people of God. The trumpet must not give an uncertain sound. *The Pulpit Commentary* has this to say about public ministry: "The ability to speak so that no one can understand us is a gift which should be earnently desired by fools only. Some men are so profound that they are quite unfathomable, even to themselves. They dig the well so deep that they drown themselves in it . . . A clear statement is like a piece of music played correctly; an involved or obscure one is like music in which the notes are all jumbled together without reference to order or time. Both may have exactly the same notes, but what a contrast." We can only exercise spiritual gift in fellowship with the church and that for the mutual benefit of all the saints.

3. THE PREPARATION FOR MINISTRY

The speaker must be conscious that he has a message from God (v. 19), *"I had rather speak five words with my understanding, that by my voice I might teach others."* It is only in malice and humility that we are to be children. In understanding we are to be men (v. 20), We must ever guard against a waste of precious time by ten thousand words to no profit. The aim of all who take public part should be to say as much as possible in as little time as possible. The most profound truths can be taught to all, if given *"in words easy to be understood."* Preliminaries and stories are both thieves of precious time. Our chapter makes it abundantly plain that the Spirit of God is more concerned with character than with gift and most jealous that Christ should be glorified and the saints edified rather than any display of human ability.

4. THE POWER OF MINISTRY

Ministry in the Holy Ghost is convincing. It flows from heart to heart. Of the listener we read, *"He is convinced of all, he is judged of all"* (v. 24). When the presence of God is felt in the midst of His people, the consciences of all are gripped. There is indeed a holy atmosphere and as the saints engage in their devotions the power of God is felt and known. It is according to the spiritual condition of the Lord's people whether they bring that power and holiness with them or not, when they come together in church. It is to be resident in each believer's life. it is possible for any one of us to resist the Spirit's power, or grieve His love or quench His light. Oh, for a deeper sensitiveness to the things that grieve Him.

> Burn, 'till there comes a daily death to every
> selfish thought.
> Burn, Thou all-consuming fire, 'till purest
> gold is wrought.

5. THE APPRAISAL OF MINISTRY

"Let the prophets speak two or three, and let the other judge" (v. 29). Ministry is tested by the judgement of the saints. No man is the judge of his own ministry. The New Testament church is characterized by a divine liberty for every member to function. But each is to function within the limits of his own capability. The dignity of the testimony is lowered by an "every-man" ministry. The assembly is solemnly responsible to God to recognize God-given gift.

The Divine Sovereignty of the Spirit of God is seen in verse 30, *"If anything be revealed to another that sitteth by, let the first hold his peace."* Here we see no chairman, no pastor presiding over the devotions of the Lord's people. All who are loyal to Divine principles will insist on the Divine Presidency of the Holy Spirit and the Divine liberty for the exercise of all God-given gift.

The movements of God in the assembly will ever lead to peace and the spirits of the prophets will be subject to each other as the Spirit of God flows through the variety of gift to the enrichment of all (vv. 32, 33).

6. DIVINE LIMITATIONS OF MINISTRY

"Let your women keep silence in the churches." In regard to our standing in the Body of Christ, there is neither male nor female, but in the local assembly the distinction between the sexes is maintained, both in dress and in position. On this important subject I quote from an article written by David McClurkin:

> Let us examine the subject of silence (of women). Two Scriptures deal with the subject (as well as the examples of the Jewish and Christian economies) 1 Timothy 2:9-15 and 1 Corinthians 14:34, 35. In Timothy the context is that of prayer. Paul, by inspiration, says that he desired men everywhere to pray. The word 'men' denotes the male of the species and does not refer merely to mankind. He then goes on to describe the ministry of women. It therefore follows that is would be inappropriate for women to speak audibly in a general meeting of the local church.
>
> In connection with the 'silence' in these two Scriptures, there are two words which perhaps give the key to its meaning. The first word is 'learn.' It is used in both of these passages. The other word is 'teach.' The word for 'teach' (cliclasko) means 'absolutely,' to give instruction (W. E. Vine) and the word for 'learn' (manthano) is related to the Greek word 'mathetes' meaning 'disciple.' The silence, therefore, referred to in these Scriptures is associated with prayer and with teaching.
>
> Paul uses another clause that may help us in the understanding of the principle he is seeking to establish — 'as also saith the law.' We would gather that he is not speaking of a peculiar situ-

ation at Corinth but rather of an order (God's order) which has been carried forward from the Old Testament to the New and hence is applicable to the church today.

What constitutes teaching? There is another Greek word used in the New Testament which is very interesting. It is the word `paideuo' which means to train children. Paul does not use this word in connection with the ministry of women. It seems clear that the teaching he refers to applies to any situation where the church is being instructed, either in doctrine or exhortation. This function is reserved for men.

Moreover, the woman as a type of the church, is not to teach. The cry of "Hear the church" is false and deceiving. It is "Hear ye Him." Christ is the Teacher and the church simply interprets the Master's voice to the world.

> Wouldst thou go forth to bless? Be sure of
> thine own ground,
> Fix well thy centre first, then draw thy circle
> round.

7. THE METHODS OF MINISTRY

"Let all things be done decently and in order" (v. 40). God lays down principles rather than rules and regulations for the guidance of His people. We may and do adopt methods to carry out the principles. But these must be in keeping with the dignity and holiness of God. In connection with this there is a word of warning in chapter 2:13, *"Communicating spiritual things by spiritual means"* (J.N.D. trans.). Only spiritual means may be used to communicate the precious things of God. What a rebuke to the frivolity of our day and what a protest to the silly things that some try to mix in with the activities of our service. Beloved saints, holiness and dignity must ever mark the testimony of the Lord.

Here then is God's simple order in which the saints function according to their several capacities. It is the place where the Lord is exalted in the midst of the congregation and where all may be edified and comforted. But when there is an abuse of gift, or an intrusion of the flesh, or a neglect of moral and spiritual suitability for the presence of the Lord, four solemn alternatives result: words spoken will not be understood (v. 2), the church will not be edified (v. 3), the saints will not be profited (v. 6), and utterances not of the Spirit will have no significance to the people of God (vv. 8-12).

The acknowledgment of the Headship of Christ is seen in chapter 11 as the preparation for keeping the weekly feast of the Lord's supper. Man takes his place in relation to Christ as Head and the woman takes her place in relation to Christ and the man. Our Lord is viewed as Head so that in all things He might have the pre-eminence (Col 1:18). He is "the Chief Musician" in our worship, the Director of all activity and the Commander-in-chief in spiritual conflict. As Head He supports every member of the Body in the perfection of His Person and work (Col. 2:19). All that dwells in Him is made available to the church. As Head He gives expression to His mind through the members of His Body on earth. His own sweet will should be our meat and drink and our every delight.

Let us sum up the teaching of these chapters with the words of the Holy Spirit: *"Let all things be done unto edifying"* (14:26); *"Let all things be done decently and in order"* (14: 40); *"Let all things be done with love"* (16:14).

> Jesus, the One who knew no sin, made sin
> to make us just,
> Thou gav'st Thyself our love to win— our
> full confiding trust.
> The mention of Thy Name shall bow our
> hearts to worship Thee;
> The Chiefest of ten thousand Thou, whose
> love has set us free.

12

Worship

In Genesis 22 three words appear for the first time in our Bible — worship, love and lamb. It is a divine association, for there could be no lamb apart from love and no worship apart from the lamb. In the first mention of a word in the Bible, often we find the key to its meaning. In the story of Abraham's going to the place of worship we have the picture of a man, who in unfeigned and loving obedience, gives his best to God.

The word "worship" is closely linked with the word "worth" or "worthiness." Abraham, with a spirit bowed in reverence, pays homage to the God of matchless worth, by yielding all to Him.

The two divine elements in worship are praise and thanksgiving. Praise is worshiping God for what He is in the Triunity of His Being, the totality of all worth, beauty and excellency. Thanksgiving is worshiping God for what He has done. God gave His best for us. His Lamb (Gen. 22) becomes our Lamb (Ex. 12). This is the order of the New Testament. God's Lamb (John 1:29) becomes our Lamb (1 Pet. 1:19, 20) when God's choice becomes our choice. Thus, the love of God, the Lamb of God and the worship of God can nevermore be separated.

Individually we should be in an attitude of worship continually. This will enable us to bring our best to God when meeting with the saints collectively. A beautiful illustration of this collective worship is seen in the priestly activity among redeemed Israel. Every Sabbath day the priest brought twelve new loaves into the holy place for the table of shewbread. These spoke of Christ, the all-sufficient One, by virtue of His atoning death, for "bread corn is bruised." God had been delighting in what the twelve old loaves typified. The priest took these home when he replaced them with twelve new ones. Thus, what God had been delighting in for seven days became the food of the priest for the next seven days. The highest aspect of worship is bringing Christ to God, in our appreciation, praise and thanksgiving. Then in return, God ministers Christ to us in fresh revelations of His beauty and worth. We bring Him home with us to share God's delights in His Son, until we meet again.

The art of presenting Christ to God is becoming a lost art. Not only the intrusion of too many hymns, with no exercise as to their place and purpose, but also an occupation with our blessings, have robbed God of much that would delight His heart. Such poverty in worship has robbed us too of the unfoldings of the beauties of Christ in the power of the Spirit, to our souls. Abraham taught his young men the art of dressing the calf, to present it to the heavenly visitors (Gen. 18:7, 8). The highest note in worship is struck when we present Christ to God. The greatest blessing is experienced when God ministers Christ to us. It is then that the Preciousness of God becomes the Preciousness of His people (1 Pet. 2:7). In the exercise of our devotional activity at the Lord's table, every function is designed to lead God's people into a deeper appreciation of the Father, the Son and the Holy Spirit.

Our Lord discusses the subject of worship with a woman in John 4. In that discussion there are some very important lessons to learn.

1. WORSHIP IS TO BE IN SPIRIT AND IN TRUTH

Judaism was a worship of the letter, ours is to be a worship of the spirit. The Samaritans' was a worship of falsehood, ours is to be in truth. Although bodily posture, ascetic rites, unholy ritual have been deemed acceptable by fallen man, in contrast to all this Christ bids us worship in spirit. The new man in Christ has had restored to him the image and likeness of God. Man's human spirit, by the power of the Holy Spirit, has now both the bias and power of honouring, praising and loving the living God. Not only is true worship through the human spirit, renewed and prostrate in the presence of God, but man, by the enlightenment of the Holy Spirit, has also a just and true conception of the God whom he worships. He worships in truth. He is able now in sincerity to experience the reality of the true God,

2. WORSHIP RESULTS FROM A TRUE KNOWLEDGE OF GOD

Our Lord mentioned three things that are essential in the soul's development in the knowledge of God:

First, God's nearness. "God is a Spirit." Shrines and images put God at a distance. They are the symbol of man's corruption of God's truth and the misinterpretation of God's Person.

> The veil is rent, lo, Jesus stands before the
> throne of grace,
> And clouds of incense from His hands fill
> all that holy place.
> Within the holiest of all, cleansed by His
> precious blood,
> Before Thy throne we humbly bow and
> worship Thee, our God.

Second, God's paternity. God is a Father, *"the Father seeketh such to worship Him."* The ritualism of Christendom destroys the beauty of this relationship When we are brought into communion with God we speak to Him as a child to his father. In all the value of His atonement our Lord Jesus ascended to introduce us to this blessed relationship; He said to Mary, when He was about to go back to the Father, *"I ascend unto my Father, and your Father; and to my God and your God."*

In the Old Testament God revealed Himself through various titles. In these we see the unfoldings of the glory of the Godhead. In the title Elohim (Gen. 1:1) we see His wisdom and omnipotence. El Shaddai (Gen. 17:1) reveals Him as the all-sufficient One who meets the need of every created thing. In the title of Jehovah there is unfolded the glory of His eternity. By this title He revealed Himself to Moses and to Israel (Ex. 6:3-6) as a covenant God. God interpreted this title to Moses when

He said, *"Say unto the children of Israel, I AM hath sent me unto you."* Again He said, *"I AM THAT I AM."* In the first we see His eternity. In the second we see His immutability. However the glory of the God of creation, the God of Abraham, Isaac and Jacob and the God of Israel, was but the glory of His back parts (Ex. 33:18-23).

It was essential that the full revelation of God's glory await the incarnation of the eternal Son. He alone could declare the Father. As the eternal Word He made the inaudible God audible, and as the eternal Light He made the invisible God visible. The shining face of Moses reflected but the back parts of God's glory. The shining face of the Lord Jesus, exalted to the Father's right hand in all the accomplishment of a finished work, unfolds the fullness of the Father's heart (2 Cor. 3:18). The sweetest aspect of that glory to us is the glory of the Father. It is the Father that seeks worshipers. Let us respond in sincere adoration.

> And now we draw near to the throne of grace
> For His blood and the Priest are there,
> And we joyfully. seek, God's holy face
> With our censer of praise and prayer.
> The burning mount and the mystic veil,
> With our terrors and guilt are gone,
> Our conscience has peace that can never fail,
> 'Tis the Lamb on high on the throne.

Third, His character. God is a Seeker. Just as the, Son seeks sinners to make them children of God, so *"the Father seeketh such to worship Him."* The notion of an unknown or unknowable God is foreign to the revelation of the Word of God. In Christ the Father is fully declared. As the Eternal Word who ever, dwelt in the bosom of the Father, He is the expression of all that was in the Father's heart. He could say, *"He that hath seen me hath seen the Father."*

In Hebrews Chapter two our Lord is seen on resurrection ground taking His place in the midst of His own redeemed people. He is seen as a Son in the midst of sons, a Priest in the midst of priests and a Worshiper in the midst of worshipers. But in all things He must have the preeminence. He is seen as the Chief Musician, the Choir Master of the church who leads the praises of the redeemed to God and our Father. Oh that we may be morally and spiritually in harmony with Him. If we are out of tune, thank God for His grace. "He will sweep across the broken strings (of our hearts) and heal the slumbering ohords again."

> His mouth the joy of heaven reveals, His
> kisses from above
> Are pardons, promises and seals of
> everlasting love.

3. WORSHIP IS TO BE INTELLIGENT

The Poor Samaritan, like others, was ignorant of true worship (v. 22). "Ye worship ye know, Ai not what." This led her to the mistaken notion that the prostration of the body in an external ritual, was both worship and reverence. But within her bosom was a proud and sinful spirit that had never been conquered. True worship is by a spirit, bowed and conquered in the presence of God, a spirit that feels his own unworthiness, yet appreciates the worthiness of God and acknowledges His justice, mercy, love and truth.

Ignorance of God and His ways leads man, through his religious and corrupt nature, into many errors. This poor woman brought the wrong spirit, Cain brought the wrong sacrifice and Nadab and Abihu brought the wrong fire. We can only worship in spirit and in truth with a deep appreciation of the Cross. Only then will the fire of true love and devotion to God burn upon the altar of the heart.

> O Lord, we know it matters not how sweet
> the song may be,
> No heart but of Thy Spirit taught makes
> melody to Thee.
> Then teach Thy gathered saints, O Lord, to
> worship in Thy fear
> And let Thy grace mould every word that

meets Thy holy ear.
Thou hast by blood made sinners meet as
    saints in light to come
And worship at the mercy seat before th'
    eternal throne.
Thy precious Name is all we show, our
    only passport, Lord;
And full assurance now we know, confiding
    in Thy Word.

In closing, may we say that unfitness for worship among the saints leads to impoverishment of soul. Of course, judicially we are fitted for worship by the worthiness of Christ, but this should lead to moral suitability for the divine Presence. Paul said to the saints at Corinth, *"Let a man examine himself and so let him eat* (of the Lord's supper)." We are all to be conscious of the truth that *"holiness becometh Thy house, O God, for ever."* Just as the people of Israel searched their homes for leaven before they partook of the passover feast, so God's people today are responsible to *"judge themselves that they be not judged."* May God help us to be better pupils in the school of God and more diligent to learn His ways. Then our holy priesthood will function more intelligently for His glory.

The fire Thy love hath kindled shall never
    be put out,
The Spirit keeps it burning (though dimmed
    by things without);
O make it burn more brightly! by faith
    more freely shine,
That we may value rightly the grace that
    made us Thine.

13

Christian Leadership

The three functional branches of assembly life may be observed in the three descriptive words, namely, Bishops, Priests and Deacons. The bishop has his authorization in spiritual maturity, the priest in spiritual birth and the deacon in spiritual gift. In this order they are identified, first, with the administration of the assembly (1 Tim. 3), second, with the intercession of the assembly (1 Tim. 2) and, third, with the doctrine of the assembly (1 Tim. 1). Each of these branches of assembly life is to function in a double capacity: oversight is to rule and to shepherd; priesthood is both holy and royal — as a holy priesthood we go in to God and as a royal priesthood we go out to men (1 Pet. 2:7,9); deaconship is related to the material and the spiritual needs of the Lord's people. We shall now look at the pattern of spiritual leadership as we see it in the Word of God.

Rule and order are important features in God's program. He made the sun to rule the day and the moon to rule the night. Governments are ordained of God for the purpose of rule. But all creature rule is subordinate to the rule of God. He is said to be the only Ruler (1 Tim. 6:15), the only Source of rule. All rule in the assembly is simply the application of the authority of God in His own house. Every leader who is God's channel in this capacity must learn first of all to rule his own spirit (Prov. 16:32). He is not to act on mere impulse, for *"the spirits of the prophets are subject to the prophets"* (1 Cor. 14:29-32).

Moreover, rule in the home is closely analogous to rule in the assembly (1 Tim. 3:5). He who rules well his own house has, at least, one good qualification for the care of the church of God.

Another feature in leadership is diligence (Rom. 12:8).

Indolence leads to disaster. There must be perpetual vigil. It is when men sleep that the enemy comes in. What a blessed example the Chief Shepherd gives us, *"Those whom Thou hast given Me I have kept and none of them is lost."* The example of the Shepherd and Bishop of our souls, is the divine pattern to which all who aspire to oversight must comform.

It is imperative when dealing with this subject that we remember the words of the Holy Spirit, *"He that ruleth over men must be just*(2 Sam 23:3). Timothy was warned by Paul to do nothing, by partiality or favor. Unjust and partial men disqualify themselves from this delicate work among the saints. Of all the moral and spiritual features that fit men for rule in the assembly the greatest ingredient is love. Love the motivating power of all true leadership. The Lord will only approve those who have it and show it. When Peter cried from the depth of a broken heart, *"Thou knowest all things, Thou knowest that I love Thee,"* Our Lord replied immediately, *"Feed lambs; feed My sheep."* Our Lord will only entrust the sheep of His pasture to the men who truely love Him.

The subject of assembly elders may be considered with regard to their designation, qualifications and duties.

1. THEIR DESIGNATION

Three words are used to help us see the internal administration of God's assembly: elder, bishop, and shepherd. Elder or presbyter suggest spiritual maturity; bishop or overseer specifies the type of their work; pastor or shepherd implies spiritual capacity. These three words describe the men who take the oversight among the Lord's people. They are not a body of legislators, for God alone legislates. They simply serve the saints in the capacity of leadership.

2. THEIR QUALIFICATIONS.

Both Timothy and. Titus, with a slight change of emphasis, lay down divine Standards for overseers. In 1 Timothy 3 the emphasis is on moral soundness, whereas in Titus 1 the emphasis is on doctrinal soundness. These qualifications relate themselves to three aspects of man's life. Inwardly, as already pointed out, he must be able to rule his own spirit (I Tim. 3:3); domestically he must be able to rule his own house (v. 4); outwardly he must bear an honest testimony before the world (v.7). Our elders, of course, are not perfect. They will always be marked by human infirmity. Therefore these qualifications are not to be used by others to demand a perfection that will and can be only known in heaven. They are simply God's ideal to which all should seek to attain.

3. THEIR DUTIES

Elders have first a duty to themselves. Three necessities pressed upon them in Acts 20:28 include, a responsibility to maintain a good spiritual condition at all times, *"Take heed to yourselves."* The mistake of the bride must be avoided, *"Other vineyards have I kept but mine own vineyard have I not kept."* Only by cultivating the holy habit of prayer and fellowship with God can we maintain a spiritual condition that is necessary for spiritual work. They are to remember that their appointment is of God, *"Over which the Holy Ghost has made you overseers."* Their appointment is neither by vote nor by self-assertion. Character and maturity are necessary to qualify for the Spirit's appointment. They are always to be conscious of the preciousness of the flock to the heart of Christ — *"The church of God, which He hath purchased with His own blood."* How precious the church should be to the undershepherds. How gentle, how tender should the saints be dealt with and always for their own good! Observe how the divine Trinity is crowded into this one verse, reminding us that any wrong done to the flock goes right to the heart of the Father, the Son and the Holy Ghost.

They have secondly, a duty to the church. Their burden is *"the care of the church"* (1 Tim, 3:5). It is interesting to note that the only other place in the New Testament where this word *"care"* is found is in Luke 10:35. The good Samaritan said to the host concerning the man that had fallen, *"Take care of him."* Every assembly should be like that inn, a place of mending, spending and tending. What reward awaits the shepherds of God's flock, *"When I come again, I will repay thee."*

There are six descriptive words in the New Testament relative to oversight duties to the Lord's dear people:

Shepherds (Acts 20:28) They are to feed the church of God. This means tend, to nourish and to support. It will include such work as visiting the sick, comforting the brokenhearted, going after the backslider, instructing the ignorant and cheering those who are discouraged by the way.

Ensamples (I Pet. 5:3) Leadership, in connection with oversight, has the thought of going before and drawing the flock after them by godly influence. It is written of godly shepherds, *"Whose faith follow, considering the end of their conversation, Jesus Christ, the same yesterday, and today, and forever"* (Heb. 13:7, 8).

Watchmen (Heb. 13:17) As such they protect the flock. Overseeing brethren are to acquaint themselves with the dangers that confront the saints. These dangers may come from without or within. They must guard the door, not only against grievous wolves from without who would creep in unawares in sheep's clothing (Acts 20:29), but also from the unruly, the vain talker and the division-maker from within (Rev. 2:2; Titus 1:10-12).

Rulers (I Tim. 5:17) The word "rule" has the thought of presiding over the flock. It is the word used for the management of a house and of children (1 Tim. 3:4, 5, 12) and the mastery of good works (Titus 3:8). The three functions of good eldership are blended in 1 Thess. 5:12: the tireless servant—*"Know them that labour among you,"* the presiding overseer—*"and are over you in the Lord,"* and the patient instructor—*"and admonish you."* Overseeing brethren, of course, have no human authority over the Lord's people. It is an authority delegated by the risen Head of the church. The rule of the assembly is the rule of God. The elders, with wisdom and love, will apply the Word to the saints. They will preside or supervise the spiritual affairs of the assembly with the delegated authority of the Chief Shepherd of the flock, enshrined in the holy Word of God.

Pilots (1 Cor. 12:28) The word *"governments"* in this verse means *"guiding the helm of affairs."* The Cambridge Bible says that it was employed in the Septuagint as the rendering of a Hebrew word signifying *"wise foresight"* (Prov. 1:5, 11:14, 22:18, 24:6). The proper meaning of the word as used here in 1 Cor. 12:28 is *"the steersman's art,"* the art of guiding aright the vessel of the church or state. As pilots, overseers are to guide or steer the assembly by wise counsel around hidden rocks that would surely cause shipwreck. We read of some, who through careless reception, were hidden rocks to cause the shipwreck of many (Jude 12).

Trustees (2 Tim. 1:14; Titus 1:9) In a general way the Word of God is committed to the church to keep and defend (Jude 3). But in a particular way leaders in the church will bear the brunt of the battle. By the Word of God they will guide the assembly and guard it against innovations that would displace its authority among the saints.

4. THEIR DANGERS

Peter points to three dangers that confront overseers (I Pet. 5). The first is **Heartlessness**, *"Not by constraint but willingly."* Godly enthusiasm in the elders will inspire God's people to greater things. Without it the assembly will lose heart and drift along like a pilotless ship. How many have lost their way through a lack of good leadership?

The second danger is **Selfishness**, *"Not for filthy lucre, but of a ready mind."* A position in the church must never be used for personal advantage. Godly men will not monopolize, either the oral ministry or the general work of God within the church. They will encourage each member to function in the place for which God has fitted him. Men who are committed to the will and interests of God, will draw the saints after them into the same current of living nobly for God.

The third danger is **Officialism**, *"Neither as being lords over God's heritage, but being ensamples to the flock."* No one man, nor any body of men, has ever been given dictatorial powers by the Lord Jesus Christ. Undershepherds rule by leadership, a leadership characterized by exemplary living. Example is better than precept and a holy life has more influence among the saints than all the power of words. Peter never forgot the lesson of John 13 when our Lord took the linen towel and girded Himself to stoop and serve. When applying the lessons to elders he says, *"Be clothed with humility"* It is only in this spirit that we can serve one another to the glory of God,

5. THEIR REWARD

If leaders among the people of God feel that they are engaged in a thankless work, let them not forget the crown of glory that will be given to those who discharge such duties to the glory of God (v. 4). Peter does not refer to the kingly crown but to the victor's wreath, the wreath of amaranth flowers that was worn by the victors in the ancient games.

6. THEIR RESPECT

Peter, having made these interesting remarks about the elders, proceeds to consider the Lord's people as a whole. He views them in their vocation as servants, soldiers and pilgrims (vv. 5-9). Linked to these three aspects of the Christian life are the three graces of humility, vigilance and patience. Grace and gift are always united in the Word of God. The great grace of humility will enable all to fit into their respective spheres and function in harmony under the guiding hand of the Spirit of God.

Three solemn responsibilities are placed upon the saints in relation to godly elders:

1. They are to recognize such and acknowledge them (1 Thess. 5:12; Heb. 13:24). This suggests that there was a recognized oversight in each New Testament church. Leadership can only replenish itself, and thus assure the perpetuation of good government in the assembly, when the door of recognition is kept open. Then as a brother matures in the things of God and the assembly discerns the characteristics of a true overseer in him, he should be acknowledged by all. The elders would then invite him to participate in the piloting of the assembly.

2. The saints are to obey the elders, submitting to godly order in the church (Heb. 13:17). Never before has the spirit of

lawlessness lifted its head so high as in our day. This spirit of the world makes inroads into our homes and into the assemblies. In some places godly oversight is displaced by a business meeting, where the vote of every novice helps to decide every matter of procedure. It was a sad day in the history of assemblies when men began to divide young from old. It is the sin of pulling asunder what God has joined together. The bitter fruits of division may be seen in many ways. Spirituality is displaced by intellectualism, spiritual gift must give way to natural ability and godly experience is of no, account in a day of dynamic personalities it is little wonder that many of God's people are unconscious of the fact that divine principles are being displaced by human innovations, and many an assembly, like a pilotless ship, is drifting toward the sea of ecumenicalism. May the Lord preserve both young and old alike from this spirit of the world. May we cultivate the great grace of humility which becomes those who are the disciples of Him who said, *"Learn of Me, for I am meek and lowly in heart, and ye shall find rest unto your souls."*

3. The assembly is to observe the devotion and sacrifice of godly leaders and follow their example (Heb. 13:7, 8). Their whole manner of life is Christ, and for His sake they serve the saints sacrificially.

The tendency to *"despise government"* (2 Pet. 2:10) is a weakness that belongs to the fallen nature of man and should be judged as such in every believer's life. Since God has ordained government for each assembly, it follows that the segregation of the saints into age groups who act independently of the elders is wrong. It is this segregation that has created such a gulf between old and young in our assembly life. The principle of the integration of all saints in the assembly life and practice is clearly seen in the early church. It is also seen in the Old Testament: *"Gather the people together, men and women and children"* (Deut. 31:10-13; Josh. 8:34). What a rebuke to those who would tear apart the integral parts of the church life of the people of God.

Some, who because of failure to keep to the simple order of God, have advocated all kinds of organization. But the Scriptures know nothing of substitutes for the pattern of God in the New Testament. The removal of all human crutches will cast us all the more upon God.

> O heavenly Father, grant us all the new-born
> babe's simplicity,
> From us the doubtful mind remove, we boast
> a God that cannot lie,
> Taught to repose, through love divine, on
> truth itself, on truth
> Thou art the Potter, we the clay, Thy will be
> ours, Thy truth our light,
> Thy love the fountain of our joy, Thine arm
> a safeguard day and night,
> Till Thou shalt wipe all tears away and bring
> forth everlasting day.

14

Deaconship

The word "deacon," derived from the Greek word *diakonia*, basically means to serve or minister. To ascertain the significance of the word we may observe several ways in which it is translated in the New Testament. In such passages as John 2:5; Matt. 23:11; Rom. 16:1, it is translated "servant." In Rom. 13:4 (twice), 15:8; 1 Cor. 3:5; Col. 1:7; 1 Thess. 3:2, it is translated "minister." From these Scriptures we learn that deaconship, like oversight, goes out in two directions. It serves the saints both in the material needs and the spiritual needs of the assembly. While there is a general service for all saints, there is a particular service that is distinguished in such Scriptures as Rom. 16:1; Eph. 3:7; Phil. 1:1; 1 Tim. 3:8. Thus there is a deaconship within a deaconship — a special service in the midst of the general service of all saints.

The church has a right to appoint its servants to look after its material needs (Acts 6:3). The risen Head of the Church alone has the right to appoint those who serve the church in its spiritual needs (Eph. 3:7). This double aspect of deaconship is seen in Acts 6:2-4. Seven men were chosen *"to serve (diakonein) tables."* But the apsotles said, *"We will give ourselves continually to prayer and to the ministry (diakonio) of the Word of God."* Serving the church in relation to its material needs is only one aspect of deaconship. The other aspect is seen in the exercise of spiritual gifts with which God has enriched His people. Thus Paul describes as deaconship the exercise both of his preaching and teaching gifts (1 Cor. 3:5; Eph. 3:7-9).

Concerning the qualifications of these responsible ministers of God, scripture indicates that a period of testing must elapse before special responsibility is entrusted: *"Let these first be proved"* (1 Tim. 3:10) and again, *"but as we were allowed (tested) of God to be put in trust with the gospel"* (1 Thess. 2:4). Men who move in and out of God's assemblies must be men of principle and character as well as men of gift. The assemblies must not tolerate anyone who fails to carry the dignity that God's standards require of responsible servants of Christ. Paul looked for three qualifications when he was about to associate with Timothy in the work of the Lord. In Timothy Paul found a man of good character, well reported of by the brethren (Acts 16:1, 2); he found a man who was endowed by the Holy Spirit with spiritual gift (2 Tim. 1.6; 7), and he was a man who was intelligent in the Word of God (2 Tim. 2:45, 3:14-17).

The wives of deacons must have qualifications as well. (1 Tim. 3:11). It is hard for any man to be any better than his wife will let him be. A woman can either make or break a man. God manifests His wisdom by insisting that the wives of trusted servants of Christ are His servants in character and godliness.

The active life of the Lord's people is beautifully illustrated by the tribe of Levi. As the Levites served under the direction of Aaron (Num. 8.:19), we serve similarly under the direction of Christ as illustrated by the seven stars that are seen in the right hand of the Son of Man (Rev. 1). Three aspects of Levitical ministry or deaconship may be observed. We read, *"At that time the Lord separated the tribe of Levi, to bear the ark of the covenant of the Lord, to stand before the Lord to minister unto Him, and to bless His name"* (Deut: 10:8). In this variety of Ministry we may see their devotional life—they ministered unto the Lord and unto Aaron (Num. 18:2), their church life—they ministered unto the congregation (Num. 16:9); and their wilderness—life they ministered unto the tabernacle (Num. 1:50). In the last aspect of their service they carried the holy vessels, with the ark alway to the forefront, a ministry in all the holy doctrines, of which the tabernacle was a type:

There were moral conditions necessary for the exereise of their ministry. When atonement was made for them, they themselves were made an offering unto the Lord (Num. 8.11). This is the pattern followed for our Levitical service in Rom. 12:1. They were then set apart for service by cleansing (Num. 8:5-13). This cleansing was fourfold—by blood, by water, by razor and by clothes. Typically this pointed to the cleansing of the conscience, the walk, the thoughts and the habits. Moral and spiritual suitability are absolute requisites for the service of the Lord.

They were then appointed to specific service (4:4, 24, 31). The three families of the Levites and their particular service point to the three aspects of the work of God today. Merari's work was foundational. At the forefront of the Levitical families they followed the ark and laid the foundation of the Tabernacle. Pioneering with the Gospel is foundational work. Paul, a true Merarite, laid foundations as he carried the Gospel into new fields and planted assemblies to the glory of God (1 Cor. 3:10). Assemblies consolidate the gains of the Gospel and established little sactuaries for God throughout the world.

Gershon's work was pastoral. They followed Merari and clothed the boards with the beautiful curtains, the colours of which set forth the beauties of Christ. Barnabas and Timothy who were true Gershonites, clothed the saints with Christ (Acts 11:22, 23; Phil. 2:20). The ministry of Christ is spiritual ministry. It can only be given by spiritual men.

The Kohathites then came with the holy vessels and put them in their proper place in the Tabernacle. This is the work of the teachers. Much damage and confusion have been wrought among the assemblies of the Lord's people by men seeking to be teachers without the ability to teach. The knowledge of one's own limitations is a great asset in assembly life. Do not we all need the grace of Barnabas who, when he had led the saints as far as his ability would take them, sought for Saul, the true Kohathite, to lead them into the ocean of divine truth. Paul and Peter were both Kohathites, with God-given gift, to set things in order in the churches (Rom. 12:6-8; 1 Pet. 4:11). No wagons were given to the Kohathites. They must bear their burdens upon their shoulders. Their work was a delicate work. Every vessel must be carried with care and put in its proper place in God's house. 1 Corinthians 12-14 describes how the vessels are put in their proper place in the house of God today. Each member was to function only in the place that God had fitted it for and appointed it to. God's order is both simple and beautiful, if we would only maintain it. The mystery of the faith is to be carried in a pure conscience (1 Tim. 3:9). God has His special men who guard the rest of a greater than Solomon in the midst of hostile forces. These men are expert in handling the Sword of the Spirit (Song of Sol. 3:7-9). The teachers among us should handle the holy doctrines of our faith with conviction and clarity. We should know what we believe and practice and defend against all corners.

> The Kohathites upon their shoulders bear
> The holy vessels covered with all care,
> The Gershonites receive another charge,
> Two wagons full of cords and curtains large;
> Merari's sons four pondrous wagons load
> The boards and pillars of the house of God.

From twenty-five to thirty years of age they served as apprentices to the work, and at fifty they retired to become overseers over the vessels of the house of the Lord. God's order cannot be improved on. God trains and tests His servants before He entrusts responsible service to them. How often have young men stepped out in the work of the Lord, professedly, as fully matured teachers before ever they served an apprenticeship in the Gospel in pioneer work. This deficiency in their experience may be hard to overcome in the years that follow. Such lack may be felt in their ministry and may lead to the danger of "trafficking in unfelt truth."

At fifty years of age they retired to the position of oversight. They were appointed to be porters which was oversight work (1 Chron. 9:26), teachers (Dent. 24:8), and leaders in song (1 Chron. 15:16-24). They were men skilled in leading the saints in worship. Stephen and Philip graduated from serving tables to serving in the Gospel and every teacher in the New Testament was first an evangelist. Let us not be ashamed to do the most menial tasks in the assembly of God's people. Remember we are "training for reigning."

All through the desert's sultry day
A weary load to carry,
Who envied them the toilsome way
Of Kohath and Merari?
Now priest and Ark alike find rest
Where God His temple raises,
And they who served with burdens pressed,
Now only serve with praises.

How perfect are the ways of God,
How just His compensation,
How low the path they humbly trod,
How high their exaltation.
No needless load on thee He'll lay,
No unrequited sorrow,
The burden-bearer of today
Is the singer of tomorrow.

— J.S. Tate

15

The Christian Priesthood

The three things that sum up the religious life of Israel in the Old Testament, the temple, the priesthood and the altar, are viewed by Peter as shadows, the reality of which is enjoyed by the church now (1 Pet. 2). In fact, his entire epistle is a revelation of the fact that the church is the inheritor of the spiritual realities of which the ritual of Israel was the type. Chapter two and verse nine sums up the contents of these five chapters, with definite references to the nation of Israel. In chapter one we are a chosen generation; in chapter two we are seen as a royal priesthood; in chapter three we are viewed as an holy nation; in chapter four we are blessed as God's peculiar people. Then in chapter five we are to show forth the excellencies of Him who hath called us from darkness into His most marvelous light.

Peter describes the priesthood of believers as both holy and royal. Thus, like oversight and deaconship, it has a double function. The burden of intercession is placed upon God's holy priesthood. We are privileged to enter the holiest by the new and living way to praise and to pray. The burden of reflection is placed upon God's royal priesthood. They are to carry the compassion of Christ to the ignorant and to those who are out of the way. Since all believers are priests, this dual responsibility falls upon all.

Mr. W. E. Vine says, "The word 'priest' originating from the Greek word 'hiereus' means one who offers sacrifice." It is used of a priest of the pagan god Zeus (Acts 14:13), of Jewish priests (Matt. 8:4, 12:4, 5; Luke 1:5) and of believers (1 Pet. 2:5,9; Rev. 1:6, 5:10, 20:6).

Let us now look at the Christian priesthood in its Possessions, its Privileges and its Prerogatives.

ITS POSSESSIONS

The priesthood of all believers has a solid foundation in Christ, the Living Stone. Its temple is a spiritual edifice, composed of living stones, adorned with the beauty of Christ. It treads the new and living way to the throne of grace, wherein is Christ, the true altar upon which spiritual sacrifices are offered and accepted by God through Jesus Christ our Lord.

The three "havings" in Hebrews ten emphasizes our rich possessions in Christ. We have a sanctuary and a way is open to it by the blood of the Cross (v. 19); we have a Great High Priest, in union with Whom we mingle our praises and intercession (v. 21); we have a double fitness, through the work of Christ and the work of the Holy Spirit, to enter into the sanctuary and minister before the Lord (v. 22). Our hearts are sprinkled from an evil conscience by the blood and our bodies are washed with pure water, indicating the washing of regeneration by the Word and the Spirit of God. The first has to do with the guilt of sin and the second with the defilement of sin. Thus, with the debt of sin cleared and its defilement gone, we draw near in full assurance of faith.

His precious blood once shed; has made and
    keeps us clean,
Enthroned in majesty the High Priest sits within;
With boldness let us now draw near,
That blood has banished every fear.

ITS PRIVILEGES

Following the three "havings" (Heb. 10) we have three exhortations, each beginning with the word "let." These are an appeal to the three lovely virtues of the "new man." Let us draw near in faith, let us hold fast in hope, let us consider one another in love (vv. 22-24; v. 23 is *hope* in J. N. D.'s translation).

The first describes our ministry before the Lord, the second our ministry before the world, and the third points to the ministry of the members one toward another to the edifying of the whole body in love. These exhortations have their illustrations in the three chapters that follow: faith in chapter eleven, hope in chapter twelve and love in chapter thirteen. There is no doubt that the writer is referring to the collective gatherings of the Lord's people, for in verse 25 he says, *"not forsaking the assembling of yourselves together."*

ITS PREROGATIVES

In the book of the Hebrews our Lord's priesthood is seen in two aspects. As the antitype of Aaron He fulfilled in His death, when He offered Himself, all that the Aaronic priesthood was typical of. As the antitype of Melchisedec He fulfills all that it was typical of in His ministry at God's right hand. The priesthood of believers is a little reflection of our Lord's. As holy priests we too have somewhat to offer, and as royal priests we too have a ministry of blessing.

We have already said that the word "priest" means one who offers. What then are the sacrifices of God's priesthood?

1. *"The sacrifices of God are a broken spirit; a broken and a contrite heart, O God, thou wilt not despise"* (Ps. 51: 17). The true meaning of the sin-offering may be learned from David's experience. There was a consciousness of his sin, it was brought to his knowledge (vv. 4, 5). This was followed by confession of the sin (vv. 3, 4). Then contrition because of the sin (v. 17), resulting in a complete break with sin (v. 19). What value God puts on broken things! Think of Gideon's broken pitcher. God blessed Jacob in the place where He broke him (Gen. 32). *"Blessed are the poor in spirit for theirs is* (the resources) *the kingdom of heaven."*

2. The sacrifices of righteousness (Ps. 4:5, 51:19). This is linked with the truth of the burnt-offering. The sin and burnt-offerings are always together. The one answers to the question of sin and the other to the question of righteousness. The Lord Jesus Christ was the Righteous One. His whole life was a continual burnt-offering, it was a sweet savour to God. The disciple

takes on the character of the Master, as he sits at His feet and drinks in of His spirit; he becomes "a sweet savour of Christ unto God" (2 Cor. 2:15).

> Be this the purpose of my soul, my solemn,
> my determined choice,
> To yield to Thy supreme control and in Thy
> kind commands rejoice.

3. The sacrifices of joy (Ps. 27:6). This is beautifully connected with the peace-offering which had to do with the happiness of God's people (Deut. 27:7). This happiness was found in worship, friendship and feasting, or joy, the fruit of reconciliation with God.

There were three varieties in this offering: a token of thanksgiving (Lev. 7:12), a vow of voluntary offering (7:16), and the heave shoulder and wave breast offering (7:14, 30). Does not this point to the three aspects of peace that we enjoy in Christ? Peace with God (Rom. 5:1), the peace of God (Phil. 4:7) and the presence of the God of peace (Phil. 4:9).

The sacrifices of thanksgiving (Ps. 116:17; Rom. 12:1; Heb. 13:15). There is no doubt that the truth of the meat-offering is before us here. It was never offered apart from the burnt-offering. Godly character is the fruit of the Cross. In all three Scriptures the mercies of God are seen in abundance. They are mercies that flow to you and me from the one great sacrifice of Christ. In the light of these mercies our lives are to be yielded to be moulded by the touch of the Master's hand. It is an act of appreciation for all the kindness of God toward us. This (our bodies) is the instrument of ten strings upon which we may bless His holy Name. If there is little praise in our souls because we have lived selfishly, let the Chief Musician, even our loving Lord, "sweep across the broken strings and heal the slumbering cords again."

> My glorious Victor, Prince Divine,
> Clasp these surrendered hands in Thine;
> Henceforth my will is all Thine own,
> Glad vassal of a Saviour's throne. —H. Moule

The sacrifices of our substance (Phil. 4:18; Heb. 13:16). One feels that we can discern the truth of the drink-offering here. The drink-offering was an act of appreciation by the offerer for all the blessings that accrued to him from the blood-offerings. Paul was willing to be poured out as a drink-offering upon the sacrificial service of the saints at Philippi (Phil. 2:17). Indeed he did this very thing for all the churches (2 Tim. 4:6). *"They first gave themselves to the Lord"* is the order in Scripture. This is followed by our possessions. What are we pouring out in thanksgiving to the Lord? Does it reach to the point of sacrifice? Our persons, our praises and our purses all belong to God by the right of purchase, and that by precious blood. All are His because He is worthy. Let us then fill the house of God with our praises and let us adorn His holy temple with a reflection of His own beauty.

> Take my silver and my gold, not a mite
> would I withhold,
> Take my intellect and use every power as
> Thou shalt choose.
> Take my love, my Lord, I pour at Thy feet
> its treasure store,
> Take myself and I will be, ever, only all
> for Thee.
> Take my hands and let them move at the
> impulse of Thy love,
> Take my feet and let them be swift and
> beautiful for Thee.

16

Discipline in the House of God

Holiness, in intelligent beings, is an aversion to sin. Every child of God is constituted a saint or holy one because God brings all His children into this pre-determined state. This position was planned and dictated by the holiness of His own nature. The "new man" in each child of God, is said to be *"created after the image of God in righteousness and holiness."* As that image is developed in each of us day by day, we are *"perfecting holiness in the fear of God."* God says, *"Be ye holy, for I am holy."* We are an holy temple in the Lord. Therefore collectively, as well as individually, we are to develop that bias toward holiness and thus give character to the assembly as the dwelling place of God.

There are three aspects of purity insisted upon by the Spirit of God in 1 Corinthians 5-7: corporate (ch. 5), personal (ch. 6) and domestic (ch. 7). Each assembly is an holy temple (ch. 3). The Spirit of God will not tolerate open sin or rebellion in God's house. The Lord's table in the assembly is a moral centre. Whether it be social impurity (ch. 5), spiritual compromise with the religious sphere (ch 10), or downright carnality (ch. 11), all are exposed and judged in the light of that centre. *"The fear of the Lord is to depart from evil."* As holiness is developed in the soul there will be a greater aversion to sin. Holiness is rectitude of character; righteousness is rectitude of conduct. If these are cultivated in the lives of God's people, they will lead to a deeper joy and satisfaction in God as well as to pure and wholesome outlook on life and its purpose.

Discipline (*sophronismos*), as Mr. W. E. Vine points out, means "saving the mind, or admonishing to soundness of mind." Its meaning is closely linked to the word "chasten" (*pai-

deuo) which Mr. Vine says primarily denotes training children, suggesting the broad idea of education. The people of God are being trained and educated for heaven. In the Word of God, all discipline has this in view. Every correction is part of our training in the ways of holiness.

There are many aspects of discipline in the Word of God. We must learn to discipline ourselves, *"for if we would judge ourselves, we should not be judged, but when we are judged, we are chastened of the Lord, that we should not be condemned with the world"* (1 Cor. 11:31,32). The Lord will correct us when we do things that are wrong so that we may learn to put a difference between clean and unclean. The assembly is to exercise discipline when that is required. God will hold an assembly responsible to judge sin that would be calculated to bring disgrace on the testimony of God. The measure of assembly discipline will depend upon the type of sin that needs to be dealt with. Moreover, all discipline must be exercised in brokenness of spirit, with a view to the recovery of the wrong-doer. Spiritual men alone should represent the assembly in this solemn work (Gal. 6:1). The one who sprinkled the water of separation on the defiled had to be clean himself (Num. 19). In that chapter there is a third day and a seventh day mentioned. Typically, the third day speaks of the resurrection of sin in the soul as the Spirit of God brings it home to the conscience. It is then that the defiled one feels the exceeding sinfulness of sin. David had such an experience (Ps. 51). In his distress he cried for the water of separation. *"Purge me with hyssop, and I shall be clean: wash me, and I shall be whiter than snow."* Then in verse 19 he entered into the seventh day experience of rest, in the assurance of restoration, *"Then shalt thou be pleased with the sacrifices of righteousness."*

We shall now look at six aspects of discipline in the Word of God:

1. THE DEFIANT

"Warn the unruly" (1 Thess. 5:14; Titus 1:10, 11). This is the sin of lawlessness. It has no relation to honest differences of opinion that may arise among saints. Honest differences lead

to inquiry, and inquiry leads to intelligence in the Word of God. But lawlessness against the established Scriptural order of the assembly is sin. The lawless one is to be deprived of the liberty of taking public part in the assembly when such activity upsets and disturbs the rest of the saints.

2. THE DISORDERLY

"Withdraw yourselves from every brother that walketh disorderly" (2 Thess. 3:6). This is another case of internal discipline. The disorderly one, according to the chapter, is one who refuses to work with his own hands. He considers that the world owes him a living, believing that it is nobody's business what he does. He is lazy and useless, with absolutely no aim in life. It is because that his testimony in the world is bringing reproach upon the assembly that the assembly must act. Each member of the local assembly should learn that what is a reproach to one is a reproach to all. Any type of disorderliness that brings reproach upon the saints would be in the same category. There are standards of holiness in God's assembly that demand action when unholy behavior begins to raise its head in the place where God has been pleased to place His Name. Withdrawal isolates the guilty one to his own behavior. He is not to be treated as an enemy, but to be admonished as a brother.

3. THE DIVISION-MAKER

"Mark them that cause division," and *"a man that is an heretic, after the first and second admonition reject"* (Rom. 16:17; Titus 3:10). The factious spirit among us is the mother of many evils. It narrows our vision, dries up the springs of our affection and withers the virtues of the "new man" so that our love cannot flow out to all the saints impartially. So enamoured does the division-maker become with the rightness of his own opinions (for which he has no *"thus saith the Lord"*) that he will press them to the point of drawing disciples after himself. All such are to be avoided, and the heretic or leader of the faction is to

be rejected after the second admonition. God's displeasure rests upon those *"who sow discord among brethren"* (Prov. 6:19). This sin is traced to the working of Satan (Rom. 16:20). If we look at the context of Romans sixteen we will see that it is in such circumstances that God reveals Himself as *"the God of peace."* Of all who imbibe His spirit, we read, *"Blessed are the peacemakers, for they shall be called the sons of God."*

4. THE DEFILED

In 1 Corinthians 5 we come to the most serious offences which call for excommunication. The man here is guilty of gross moral evil. Linked with this are other sins that call for the extreme penalty (v. 11). The Corinthian saints were so out of touch with God that they had lost their priestly prerogatives of vision, touch and smell. They were unconscious of the fact that sin, like leaven, was rampant and permeating the whole. Paul commands with apostolic authority that the assembly be cleansed. When the assembly assumes its proper responsibility it acts in three ways: the first step is judicial when sin is exposed (vv. 1-5), the second step is spiritual when sin is purged (vv. 6-8), and the third step is social when the guilty is put away (vv. 9-13). It is to be noted that the carnal condition of the church as a whole made it easy for the devil to take advantage of them. The safety of God's people lies in keeping in fellowship with God. As we abide in Him "the devil toucheth us not."

5. THE DOCTRINAL

Wholesome doctrine and conduct are united in the Word of God. Loyalty to the "historic faith of God's elect" is basic and fundamental to Christian fellowship. The evil teacher is to be refused social intercourse in the home (2 John) and is to be put away from the assembly (1 Tim. 1:19, 20; 2 Tim. 2:17, 18). It does matter a great deal what we believe. The preservation of the assemblies of the Lord's people depends on sound doctrine. Assemblies must not, on the peril of their own safety, look lightly on the departure all around them. This departure, we fear, has already started in certain groups that once claimed assembly ground. Brethren, let us beware! Indifference to truth and a disregard for the rights of God in His own house will bring His displeasure upon us. The craze for change among us has led to tampering with divine principles. The great religious ecumenical movement in the world is both subtle and deceptive and many of God's people are being drawn into this devilish quagmire. Our path is "outside the camp" unto our rejected Lord. Where the Word of God has clearly defined our path, let us walk in it. Let us love our Lord fervently and be loyal to His truth. Remember the imbalance in the church at Ephesus; she hated evil yet had left her first love. We can only hate evil with a holy hatred when we are loving our Lord with a fervent love.

6. THE DISTURBER

"Let him be unto you as an heathen man and a publican" (Matt. 18;15-18). This is the incorrigible offender who has wounded his brother. In spite of the wrong done to the innocent one, that brother seeks to win back the offender, approaching him in the spirit of the kingdom of heaven. This is the spirit of humility (v. 4), of godly care (vs. 12, 13), of peace (vs. 15-18) and of brotherly forgiveness (vs. 21-34). However, the disturber refuses every overture to be reconciled to the offended one. This procedure binds his sin upon him, and what is bound by the Word of God on earth is bound by the will of God in heaven. He is no ordinary offender. His picture is drawn by our Lord in the parable that follows. He has brought the spirit of the heathen into a sphere in which the spirit of the kingdom of heaven alone should prevail. Until he puts it right with his brother whom he has grievously injured, he must be prepared to go through life without the comfort of the fellowship of God and His people. As the heathen man and the publican are outside the assembly, so must he be while his sin is unconfessed. To persist in such a course will inevitably lead to grief (v. 34). We have lived long enough to see hard and unforgiving men die in the hand of the tormentors.

What a holy place God's temple is! Oh, that His fear may be

upon us lest we bring reproach to His holy Name and grieve His beloved people.

While each assmbly has the obligation, if necessity arises, to exercise discipline within the confines of its own local fellowship, it has no commandment from the Lord to excommunicate another assembly of the Lord's people. Discipline is commanded for individuals, not for companies. On this subject Mr. John Ritchie, the late editor of the Believer's Magazine, has this to say:

> We have no authority from the Lord to excommunicate an assembly of the Lord's people. The Lord retains this form of discipline in His own power. When He disowns any church of His because of continued and aggravated dishonour of His Name and disloyalty to His truth (Rev. 2:5), it will become so manifest that *all the churches shall know'* (v. 23) what has been done and bow to the divine judgement, or if not, ultimately share it. But no individual or groups of individuals, no church or group of churches, has the work delegated to them by the Lord, to disown, or cut off, or excommunicate entire companies of fellow-believers, even though they may reckon that they are not loyal to certain truths plainly taught in the Word. If their consciences, governed by Scripture, do not permit them to go in and out with such, then let them refrain, but always distinguish between those who are leaders in wrong, who have embraced the evil, and those who, while not strong enough to protest against it, are yet reckoned by the Lord not to be participators in it. They are *those who have not the doctrine'* and are not charged by Him with having it, although reproved for lack of faithfulness in suffering it in others (v. 20).
>
> Like the suspected leprous house (Lev. 14:34, 35), a period of patient waiting and watchfulness

— and surely prayful and deep exercise of heart among all *'who watch for souls'* and seek the godly welfare of fellow-saints in so dangerous a position — must be given. Should restoration of the whole be proved impossible, even then the Lord's way is *'to make a difference'* (Jude 22-24) between leaders in the evil and the simple ones who follow, taking *'the precious from the vile'* by a ministry which, as from the mouth of the Lord (Jer. 15:19), divides, as with a two-edged sword, what is of God from that which is opposed to Him.

Refraining from going to any place or company in which confidence has been lost, is a matter for the individual to decide as before the Lord. But unless, and until the Lord Himself has made it so plain (and in many well-known cases He has, to all who have godly discernment) that He has disowned an assembly of His, any company that assumes that place and has borne that Name, it is not for us to issue any decree that this or that is not to be regarded any longer as God's assembly.

A godly intelligence in the Word of God will lead us to distinguish between leaving an assembly alone that is determined to pursue a wrong course and cutting an assembly off. Although we may leave an assembly alone because of its indifference or opposition to divine principles of assembly life and practice, yet our attitude should always be that of a readiness to help the wayward when their course of departure is reversed. But to cut off an assembly is to abandon it beyond all hope of recovery. Let our attitude be as our Lord who, in the midst of the seven churches, sought the recovery of the wayward and only removed the lampstand when all hope of recovery was gone.

Thou, our heavenly Master, bid contentions cease,
Thou, true Prince of Salem, give Thy children peace;
Peace from God the Father, peace from God the Son,
Peace from God the Spirit, Jehovah three in One.

17

Christian Separation
2 Corinthians 6

Paul, in the Corinthian letters, seeks to warn the saints of two snares of the wicked one. In the first letter he points out that the Devil divides what God has united — the people of God. In the second letter he shows that the Devil unites what God has separated — the church and the world. To know the strategy of Satan will help to fortify us against his attacks.

Second Corinthians 6 is the greatest treatise on Christian separation in the New Testament It begins with the receiving of the grace of God. When this is received aright it will produce holiness. To receive it in vain is to refuse to put it to work. Christianity is the most unselfish thing in the world. The people of God are to be monuments of that unselfishness. When we receive the grace of God we are to pass it on to others in God's accepted time, the day of His salvation (v. 2). This means that separation is not isolation. Isolation is a cold thing. Monuments to that philosophy may be seen in the convents and monasteries of the world or in the heretical Taylor party of Exclusives. Isolation is a cold physical withdrawal unto asceticism. True separation is a warm spiritual dedication unto the Lord. Eight times over in Numbers 6 we read that the separation of the Nazarite was *"unto the Lord."* The word *"sanctification"* has this double meaning. It is not only a separation from what is defiling, but a separation *"unto the Lord."* We read of the Lord Jesus Christ that *"He was holy, harmless, undefiled and separate from sinners."* Yet His contacts with the unsaved were warm and loving and true.

No wonder that little children, in all their innocence, and penitent sinners, in all their guilt, were alike drawn to Him in a most mysterious way, while the self-righteous Pharisee recoiled from Him with murmuring and hate. Separation therefore is not from contact with sin, but from fellowship with sin.

Having stated that we are workers together with God (v. 1), he now says (v. 4) that we are to commend ourselves by characters that are transformed by the power of God. The message of reconciliation that is committed to us to preach (5:20), will only be acceptable to men when the power of that message is evident in our own lives. The power of this transfiguration (3:18) will be seen in three ways: first, in the circumstances of everyday life where character is tested by adversity (6:4, 5). Note the nine things that test the physical endurance of the saints: afflictions, necessities, distresses, stripes, imprisonments, tumults, labours, watchings and fastings.

Second, it will be seen in our attitude to adversity (vv. 6-7). All adversity is meant to develop and bring into practical manifestation the virtues of the "new man." Note the nine things that are tested in the spiritual endurance of the saints: pureness, knowledge, longsuffering, kindness, the Holy Ghost (in full control), genuine love, the word of truth, the power of God and the armour of righteousness.

Third, it will be seen in the path that we are called upon to tread to the glory of God (vv. 8-10). Here again there are nine things mentioned as the spectators of heaven and earth give their verdict: honour and dishonour, evil report and good report, deceivers yet true, unknown and yet well known, dying and behold we live, chastened yet not killed, sorrowful yet always rejoicing, poor yet making many rich, having nothing yet possessing all things.

Paul, though treading a narrow path, had a large heart (vv. 11, 12). He says, as it were, *"our hearts are large enough to receive you and give you our affections, but yours are too narrow to receive us."* What a contrast, a man of God with a large heart and a worldly church with a narrow heart. Godly separation unto the Lord leads to largeness of heart, but worldly sectarianism dries up the springs of our affections so that they cannot flow out to all the saints impartially. Paul, by the Spirit, cried, *"Be ye also enlarged."*

Open your hearts to the people of God and close them to the world. This does not mean that we are to embrace evil principles that hold many saints in sectarian folds. It simply means that our hearts are to be open to all saints as members of the one body of Christ, while, at the same time we seek to walk in simple paths, outside all denominational folds, in fellowship with a rejected Christ.

Let us remember that in holding the truth of God, we hold it as the property of all saints. If a brother seeks for that which he has lost, then we must restore it to him (Deut. 22:1). Thus, the assemblies meeting on New Testament lines should be an attraction to godly saints who, when tired of the sham and departure of Christendom, seek for rest for their souls among the people of God. But if the assemblies pursue the trend toward interdenominationalism and ecumenicalism they will not fulfill the role for which they exist, in the purpose of God. They will also lose the high privilege of being custodians of the truth of God in all its purity and the joy of welcoming exercised saints who are tired of the religious confusion and corruption all around them.

Paul now points to five aspects of Scriptural separation:

The Commercial *"What fellowship hath righteousness with unrighteousness?"* Money is called *"the mammon of unrighteousness."* Of course we must do business in the world and with the world. But we must not enter into any business partnership with the ungodly. There can be no fellowship with the men of the world without irreparable harm to our spiritual life and testimony. The principles that govern the world and the principles that govern the Lord's people are diametrically opposed.

The Political *"What communion hath light with darkness?"* We read of *"the rulers of the darkness of this world."* Governments, while ordained of God to maintain law and order in every land, are nevertheless influenced and guided by spiritual wickednesses in high places. The saints are destined to judge the world to come and must not reign as kings before their time. However much of the salt of truth there is in governments, it is the result of the influence of Christianity on the hearts of men.

The Social *"What concord hath Christ with Belial?"* Society has its own head, which is Satan. Its joys and satisfaction depend on the exclusion of Christ. How can a child of God be yoked with anything whose life and movements exclude our blessed Lord? Our Lord has already warned us that the place that society gave Him is the place it will give His people. But would we want to be where our Lord is undesired?

The Matrimonial *"What part hath he that believeth with an unbeliever?"* Nothing but sorrow and grief can follow disobedience to this law. Let our young men and women beware of this snare of the Devil. Many choice saints of God have been brought down to grief and remorse by falling for this temptation. Marry only *"in the Lord"* and the blessing of God will follow you into this blessed union.

The Religious *"What agreement hath the temple of God with idols?"* Israel was to meet only *"where the Lord had placed His Name."* This was to save them from religious confusion and corruption by bringing them under the control of the Word of God. The place for every Christian is where the Word of God rules in all the public exercises of the saints and where the Lord alone is the Centre.

What participation then, what affinity of spirit, what harmony of thought, what blending of interests, what unity of devotion can the church have with the world? *"Come out from among them"* is God's command to His people.

But separation is not only from, it is unto the Lord. When we learn both sides of this blessed truth it will be warm and satisfying. We will "sit under His shadow with great delight and His fruit will be sweet to our taste."

Paul points to three aspects of this fruit that await those who come out unto the Lord:

a. It brings us closer to God, *"I will receive you and be a Father unto you."* God will then be able to lavish all His love and protection upon us. He will reveal His will and purpose and make our lives a bright reality for Him in this dark world of sin.

b. It will bring the saints closer to one another, *"Ye shall be my sons and daughters saith the Lord Almighty."*

That is to say, family affection will become more apparent and Christian fellowship all the more sweet.

c. It will bring God closer to us, *"I will dwell in them and walk in them and I will be their God."* Here we see the indwelling God, the active God and the controlling God. Ephesus put Christ out of the heart. Laodicea put Him out of the door. But oh, the graciousness of our Lord! He knocks for admittance. He longs to come into our lives, into our homes and into the assemblies. Here is the price we must pay: give up the world or part with the conscious presence of our adorable Lord.

> Rise, my soul, thy God directs thee, stranger
> hands no more impede,
> Pass thou on, His hand protects thee, strength
> that has the captive freed.
> Art thou weaned from Egypt's pleasures? God
> in secret thee shall keep,
> There unfold His hidden treasures, there His
> love's exhaustless deep.

Not only will we taste the sweetness of His presence, but we will see His movements among us, *"I will walk in them."* The footsteps of God will be seen in the activities of the saints. We will be able to say like Jacob of old, "God is in this place — the house of God." Even the visitor who occupies the seat of the unlearned will be able to say as he watches the exercises of the saints, *"God is in you of a truth."*

The control of God is another aspect of this fruit, *"I will be your God."* The acknowledgment of the authority of God brings sweet harmony to our lives, our homes and our assemblies. Anything less than this will only lead to chaos and grief.

"Having therefore these promises, dearly beloved" (7:1). What promises? The promise of the indwelling God, of the active God and of the governing God. What then? *"Let us cleanse ourselves from all filthiness of the flesh and spirit, perfecting holiness in the fear of God."* Holiness is our vocation. We have been *"called unto holiness."* In the purposes of God toward us we as His people are to develop along four lines of holiness.

First, we are holy brethren (Heb. 3:1). Holiness is to be developed in our relationships with each other. As we grow in our aversion to sin, we will be careful not to hurt the people of God. We will cultivate the spirit of brotherly forgiveness and shun like the plague all bitterness and petty jealousies.

> If a little word of mine, perhaps unkind or
> untrue,
> Would leave its trace on a loved one's face,
> I would not utter it, would you?

> But if a little thought divine would linger the
> whole day through,
> And lift the heart with a heavier part,
> I would not withhold it, would you?

Second, we are a holy priesthood (1 Pet. 2:5). We are to be holy in all our devotions. *"Who shall ascend into the hill of the Lord? Who shall stand in His holy place? He that hath clean hands and a pure heart. Who hath not lifted up his soul unto vanity and hath not sworn deceitfully. He shall receive a blessing from the Lord and righteousness from the God of his salvation"* (Psa. 24). The fear of the Lord will lead us to tread softly in the courts of the Lord and godly reverence will become us in every exercise in the assembly of His people.

Third, we are an holy temple. *"The temple of God is holy, which temple ye are"* (1 Cor. 3:17). We are to be holy in all our behaviour. The temple of God is either adorned or defiled by individual behaviour. Each believer brings into the assembly of God a life that will either add to the joys of God's people or contribute to their griefs. *"Take heed to thyself"* is a warning to each of us, for holiness is not only desired but it is commanded by God.

Fourth, we are an holy nation (1 Pet. 2:9). We are to be holy in our testimony before the world. Oh, for a greater sensitiveness to sin and a deeper knowledge of God. How we long for a greater capacity to interpret Him to men in the harmony of the two aspects of His holy character, God is light and God is love. We can only do it in the measure that these have a reflection in our own lives, as we grow in grace and in the knowledge of our Lord Jesus Christ.

Then let us, brethren, while on earth with foes
  and strangers mixed,
Be mindful of our heavenly birth, our
  thoughts on glory fixed.
That we should glorify Him here, our Father's
  purpose is,
Whene'er the Saviour shall appear, He'll fully
  own us His.

18

The Lord's Work
And its Financial Support

Every young believer should learn his financial responsibility to the Lord's work. The art of systematic giving should begin early in the Christian life. It is one of the joys of our Christian life to lay aside at least one-tenth of our income exclusively for the Lord. This does not involve being brought under the law of Moses. Tithing was in practice long before the law was given. It is a part of the established order of God for His people in all dispensations. Even those in full-time service should follow the example of the Levites who received tithes and gave tithes (Num. 18:25-32). This not only brings present joy into our lives, but it also brings blessing to our substance (Prov. 3:9, 10; 11:24; 2 Cor. 9:10) and adds treasure to our account in heaven (Phil. 4:17).

There are collective obligations to be met in fellowship with the assembly (Acts 11:29, 30; Rom. 15:25-27; 1 Cor. 16:1, 2). There is also the personal exercise before the Lord to give privately (3 John 5-7; Gal. 6:6; 1 Tim. 5:18). This leads to a greater exercise in prayer as to where our fellowship should go, as well as to increase our burden for the work that God is doing through others. God is glorified in our giving and we ourselves are brought into subjection to the claims of the Gospel (2 Cor. 9:13, 14).

Collective giving occurs on the first day of the week when the saints are gathered in assembly capacity (1 Cor. 16:1, 2). Thus it becomes a part of our worship, symbolizing our appreciation of our wonderful Lord.

Public offerings at gatherings where the unsaved are invited to hear the Gospel are unknown in the New Testament. In this we obey the words of the Lord Jesus, *"Freely ye have received, freely give."* This principle applies to the Sunday School as well as to any other public meeting.

It is a sad reflection of a carnal condition when so many of God's people, like silly sheep, are ready to run after every new thing that emerges. Money is poured into great projects, many of which are a direct infringement on divine principles. As God's people are, drawn more and more into interdenominationalism we may well see more of these methods copied from the religious world.

Let us tread the path of divine simplicity. Our preservation and safety, as New Testament assemblies, lies in our separation and loyalty to the Word of God. Our distinctive testimony to the whole truth of God can only be maintained by refusing to be conformed to the world around us.

WORDS OF COUNSEL TO THOSE WHO SERVE THE LORD

One of the greatest privileges to be conferred upon us is to be called of God into specific service. To know God is to love Him, and to love Him is to serve Him. But privileges bring their corresponding responsibilities. With that in view let us weigh carefully the following remarks.

Those in full-time service are to go forth *"taking nothing of the Gentiles."* Depending on the Lord alone, they are to tell their needs to none but the Lord Himself. Circular letters with hints for support, or public announcements of needs, are foreign to the New Testament pattern. It is to the credit of the assemblies' testimony that in the past they have carried on the work of God with no appeals whatever for money. Alas, in our day, there is even departure in this. Our homes are flooded with mail appealing for money for certain, professedly, assembly projects. Such men have never learned the ways of God.

One safeguard for the protection of the assemblies lies in careful commendation. The greatest commendation one can have is his own character and ministry. This should be apparent to all the Lord's people. Anyone who is not acceptable in his own home assembly and in the assemblies in his own immediate vicinity will never be acceptable nor useful anywhere else. Elder brethren should not irresponsibly commend such, thus putting an intolerable burden on assemblies elsewhere, either at home or abroad.

Our Lord fashions His servants in secret for what He wants them to be in public (Isa. 49:2). The apostles were in the company of our Lord for three to four years, imbibing His spirit and character and learning His ways in the work of God. They were first disciples, then evangelists and then teachers. This is God's order. Moses sought to be a leader in Israel before he matured in the school of God in the backside of the desert, but God rejected him. Elisha had to walk with Elijah learning his ways before the mantle fell upon him. Paul was sent into Arabia to learn God. Then he spent some years in Tarsus, his home district, before going to Antioch, from whence he was recommended to the grace of God (Acts 13:1-3). He himself testified, "After I was tested, I was put in trust with the gospel" (1 Thess. 2:4).

The assembly, with its privileges and activities, is the best training ground for God's servants. Here young believers may sit under a variety of ministry by godly and gifted servants of Christ, both local and itinerant. There is opportunity to engage in every branch of its work such as open-air meetings, Sunday School, tract distribution, etc. There is also the benefit of wise counsel from godly elders, providing opportunity of maturing in an atmosphere where "thus saith the Lord" is paramount. God has no substitute for this. As one learns God in the secret of His own presence, and the ways of God in fellowship with His people in the assembly, he may put it into practice in the circumstances of everyday life, whether in the office, the factory, the high school or the university. This leads to strength of character and a stable personal testimony for Christ.

Scripture says, "Know them that labour among you." The Lord's people have the right to know what manner of men move in and out among them. What is their character? Are they Christian gentlemen, both in ministry and behaviour? Or are they exacting, inconsiderate and unmannerly? What is the value of their ministry? Have they won souls to Christ and established the saints in the right ways of the Lord? What are their motives? Are they in the work for the glory of God or for filthy lucre, the praise of men, or an easy, aimless life of travel at the Lord's people's expense?

The principles by which assemblies function are spiritual principles and can only operate aright when there is spirituality among the Lord's people. It is possible (and indeed it happens) that because we have no board of directors or centralized authority, that those out in full-time work become a law unto themselves. Therefore in the absence of a tender conscience and personal devotedness to the Lord, one may make the preaching or missionary profession an excuse for a lazy, aimless existence, using the assemblies as a tramping ground for touring the world. (We are not referring to gifted men of God who have a universal ministry for the churches of the saints.) It is possible to settle on a mission station, doing nothing except to hinder the native believers from assuming their proper responsibilities in the local assemblies. It is possible to become a weekend preacher, with neither a burden for the lost nor a care for the weary and poor of the flock. Mr. Harold St. John once said that when one is working for an earthly master he will give him at least eight hours a day. When working for our heavenly Master we should give Him no less. This Christian gentleman divided his own day into three parts: the morning for prayer, study and writing; the afternoon for visiting, and the evening for preaching.

It is because divine principles can only succeed when working through spiritual channels, that the assemblies should be doubly careful to see that only godly, devoted and indispensible servants should be released for full-time work. Trace the path of godly servants of Christ in the Acts. It is indispensible men that are called (13:1-3). They did not make a tour of assemblies to tell what they were going to do, but plunged right into the work of preaching the Gospel and planting assemblies. Then after a while they returned to their home assembly to declare what the Lord had wrought (14:26, 27). Follow their path and see how they were completely under the Spirit's control: *"They were forbidden of the Holy Ghost to preach the word in Asia"* (Acts

16:6), teaching us that the need of any country does not constitute a call to go. *"The Spirit suffered them not," "a vision appeared
unto Paul in the night."* Here doors open and close to them as
they move in the path of the will of God. There are three conver-
sions in the chapter that laid the foundation for the first assembly in Europe. Each soul needed a different approach. But men
trained in soul-winning will find the approach to broken hearts.
The first is the picture of a seeking soul (v. 14), the second of a
deceived soul (vv. 16- 18) and the third of the out and out sinner
(vv. 30, 31). Note the equipment that was used in these conver-
sions: in the first instance the emphasis is on the Word of God,
in the second it is on the Name of Christ and in the third it is
on the power of the Holy Spirit. Such equipment is better than
Saul's armour to meet the giant who holds souls in bondage.
We must let this emphasis remain. There can be no substitute
for the Word of God, nor for the authority of Christ enshrined
in His lovely Name, nor for the power of the Holy Ghost.

Moreover, each servant is to carry out the full commission
of our Lord in Matthew 28. Let us observe first of all a false
commission in the chapter. It has been observed that this false
commission of the elders and priests to the soldiers consisted
of three things: they were sent forth to preach a dead Christ,
to proclaim a lie, and large money was to be paid to them. In
the true commission of our Lord the disciples were sent forth
to preach a living Christ, to proclaim the whole truth, and not
one word was spoken about money. They were sent forth in
dependence on God and their needs were to be told to Him
alone. Shame on any servant whether at home or abroad, who
leaves the path of faith to look to men. Let us remember that he
who pays the piper will call the tune. To be bought with money
means to be governed by the buyer. Every servant of Christ, if
he wants to keep his fellowship with God, must be clear and
definite about this fact, that any gifts that are sent him with
strings attached, he must resolutely refuse, for God will only
honour them who honour Him.

There are three things joined together in our Lord's commission that we dare not put assunder. They were to make
disciples out of all nations; they were to **mark** disciples in the

waters of baptism, and they were to mould disciples by the teaching of the whole Word of God. This commission was carried out to the letter in the Acts of the Apostles: they made disciples (14:21, marg.), they baptized believers only (2:41; 8:12, 38; 9:18; 10:47; 16:15, 33; 18:8; 19:5) and they established them in local assemblies to be moulded by the Word of God (Rom. 6:17, New Trans.). When they had taught the converts they appointed elders or overseers in every church. Then they placed on the shoulders of the converts the responsibility to function and witness. This left the saints free to develop along responsible lines, working out their own salvation in the fear of God (14:23; Phil. 2:12). It is true that the apostles returned to minister to these assemblies. This was not to do their work for them, however, but to equip them to do their own work better (Eph. 4:11-16) .

There are four "alls" in the commission. Our Lord said, *"All authority is given unto Me."* That means that He alone has the right to command, to control and constrain us. This authority He will not share with another. In the realm of a scripturally instructed conscience, Christ must reign supreme.

"Teach all nations." This suggests that the world is the parish of the church. The gift of tongues in the early church was given as a sign to the Jewish nation that it had refused to share the knowledge of God *"with men of other tongues"* (Isa. 28:11, 12; 1 Cor. 14:21). The church is now called to be God's public witness to men. We are responsible to give the Gospel to the people of every language. This is the debt we have to discharge to the world. We thank God that one thing the church has excelled in above all others is in the learning of languages. Today the Gospel goes out to all the world and the Word of God is translated into most languages.

"All things" point to the creed of the church. It is the whole Word of God. It contains our marching orders. It alone is to guide us in the way the work of God should be done. Paul said, *"As a wise master builder I have laid the foundation"* (1 Cor. 3). He was simply the superintendent of the blueprints. He saw the pattern of God's assembly at Corinth in laying the first stone. Elder brethren should make sure that each one commended to full-time service is acquainted with the pattern of the New Tes-

tament assembly. He should know the commission and carry it out to the full. He should beware of the snare of clericalism, "which thing the Lord hates." He should be sufficiently intelligent in the Word of God to teach the converts to assume responsibilities in priesthood, ministry and eldership and then to step aside, permitting the faith of the saints to work. Distinguished gift, we must emphasize again, is given, not to do the work of the saints for them, but to equip them to do their own work. A knowledge of this divine principle in the Lord's work would save us from the spirit and methods of the religious world, thus leading to healthier indigenous churches of the saints.

"All your days" is a promise that vouchsafes to the church the presence of her Lord until the day of her testimony is ended. In this lovely promise we have the companionship of a Friend, the watchfulness of a Guard and the guidance of an Eye that neither slumbers nor sleeps.

I shall close this chapter with the words of a devoted servant of the Lord:

> The want of the age is men. Men of thought. Men of action. Men who are not for sale. Men who are honest to the heart's core. Men who will condemn wrong, whether it be in friend or foe, in themselves or in another.
>
> Men whose consciences are as true as the needle of the compass is to the pole. Men who will stand for the right though they stand alone. Men who can tell the truth and look the world right in the eye.
>
> Men whose courage comes from within and whose joy springs from the soul's deep fountain. Men through whom the current of everlasting life runs still and deep and strong. Men too large for certain limits and too strong for the bondage of men. Men who know their message and tell it. Men who know their place and fill it. Men who are not too lazy to work, nor too proud to be poor. Men — real men of God.

God give us men, a time like this demands it,
Strong minds, great hearts, true faith and ready hands;
Men whom the lust of office does not kill,
Men whom the spoils of office cannot buy;
Men who possess opinions and a will,
Men who have honour, men who will not lie;
Men who can stand before a demagogue
And disdain his treacherous flatteries without winking.
Tall men, suncrowned, who live above the fog,
In public duty and in private thinking;
For while the rabble with their thumb-worn creeds,
Their large professions and their little deeds,
Mingle in selfish strife, Lo! freedom weeps,
Wrong rules the land and waiting justice sleeps.

—Josiah G. Holland

19

Inter-assembly Relationship

In a day of confusion and division, the subject of the fellowship of assemblies is a most delicate one to approach. We shall try to discuss it in the fear of God and with a regard for the vindication of the truth alone.

On both sides of our divided house there are extreme views pressed upon the saints by certain leaders. On the one side there seems to be a determination to support the great ecumenical movement, in order to become more popular with the religious world. Interdenominationalism, with its recognition of the clerical system, is becoming common This inevitably leads to the copying of such sectarian ways and methods as the reception of clerical men to assembly platforms, the employment of a one-man pastor and the acceptance of the theological seminary. Companies of God's people that have gone back to such unscriptural practices, face the danger of forfeiting their place as New Testament assemblies.

On the other side there is the assumption of high ecclesiastical claims with a Diotrephes' spirit that, without respect to moral or doctrinal considerations, casts out of the assemblies godly and conscientious children of God. In the great division between Muller and Darby, the assembly in Bristol insisted on making a distinction between leaders who erred and the innocent of the flock. Such a distinction has been urged by godly brethren ever since.

We shall now look at the fellowship of assemblies as it is portrayed in the Word of God.

1. IT IS A FELLOWSHIP OF LIFE

Since every church epistle is written to a congregation of saints, the mixture of saved and unsaved is unknown in any New Testament church. The scriptural order is: salvation, baptism and reception to the local assembly. Each church had a recognized fellowship comprised of the people of God alone. The following statements make this abundantly clear: *"unto the church of God at Corinth, sanctified in Christ Jesus, called saints"* (1 Cor. 1:2), *"to all that be in Rome, beloved of God, called saints"* (Rom. 1:7), *"to the saints that are in Ephesus and to the faithful in Christ Jesus"* (Eph. 1:1). This would surely demand a reserved seat for the unsaved when the saints meet at the Lord's table. It would also demand carefulness on the part of elder brethren to look for signs of divine life in every professor when he is examined for baptism and reception to the local assembly.

2. IT IS A FELLOWSHIP OF LIGHT OR TRUTH

There was intercommunication of truth among all the churches of the saints. The epistles of truth were to be read in all the churches (Col. 4:16), the contents of which were binding on all (1 Cor. 4:17; 7:17). No assembly could keep its fellowship with other assemblies if it departed from the basic fundamentals of true Christianity.

Scriptural customs that were taught by apostolic authority were binding on all the churches. This was true of Christian deportment and dress. The distinctions in dress and place between male and female were to be permanently maintained, not only because of the dignity of God's house, but because of their spiritual lessons to angels and to us (1 Cor. 11: 3-16; 14:34, 35).

This uniformity in the churches was also true in regard to finances. All were taught how and when to support the widow, the poor and the work of the Lord. We know that uniformity is not unity. But what is wrong with uniformity when it is the result of a common obedience? It is nice to be able to say, when something foreign to our assembly life is being pressed by some who have a craze to change everything, *"We have no such custom, neither the churches of God"* (1 Cor. 11:16).

Questions that affected all the Lord's assemblies were to be discussed at a conference of elder brethren (Acts 15). As a result of the conference all the churches were advised that nothing was to be done that would offend the consciences of other saints. Does this not teach us that the principles that govern individual behavior (Rom. 14) are the same that are to govern the behavior of assemblies one toward another? The exclusive system of assemblies pressed their unity to the point of confederacy. We on the other hand, have carried independency to the point of confusion. Truth usually lies between extremes. The truth of the autonomy of each assembly was never meant to be carried to the point of independency. There is a fellowship of assemblies, based upon a common loyalty to our risen Lord and a humble submission to the binding power of His holy Word. Before any new thing is introduced in any assembly, certain questions should be asked: Will it violate any principle of the Word of God? Will it lead to a conflict of opinion in the assembly, thus grieving the Spirit of God? Will it maintain the dignity of God's house? Will it offend other assemblies with whom happy fellowship has existed? If so, then God will not bless such an innovation, and they who persist in it must bear their burden before the Lord.

THE AUTONOMY OF EACH ASSEMBLY

In government, each assembly stands upon its own base, responsible to the Lord alone. In fellowship, each is interdependent, as all are necessary to bear a competent testimony to the Lord. In the letters to the seven churches (Rev. 2, 3), each assembly stood upon its own base, but all seven threw their united rays upon the One who walked in the midst of the churches. Each letter was written to meet a particular need in a particular church, yet all seven letters were binding upon all the saints (2:29). Each church had a recognized government (Phil. 1:1), answerable to the Lord alone. But in gift and testimony only the whole body is sufficient in itself (Eph. 4:1-16). When one assembly is weak, help may come from another assembly (Acts 11:19-26).

While fellowship among assemblies is clearly taught in the Word of God, a union or confederation of assemblies is not taught. This is the error upon which beloved brethren of the Exclusive system stumbled. On this subject the late Mr. George Goodman wrote, "Fellowship with other assemblies is maintained, but it is the fellowship of the Spirit and not of a party. One assembly must refuse to accept orders from another or from any body of men. This not only maintains the unity of the Spirit, but is also a safeguard in days of persecution which soon may be upon us. If we were organized under an earthly head the enemy would know where to strike. However, if we remain as autonomous assemblies of the saints, the blow that scatters one, only leads to the scattered members forming other assemblies wherever they are driven, as in the case of the persecution under Saul of Tarsus" (Acts 8:4).

3. IT IS A FELLOWSHIP OF LIBERTY

We have already said that no assembly is bound by edicts from any central authority. Each assembly is to act before the Lord, in accordance with His holy Word — its only guide. The Word of God teaches principles of truth for each assembly to follow. However, the Word does not legislate methods of procedure for carrying out those principles, but every method must be in keeping with the dignity of those principles, never infringing upon them.

Unfortunately many methods adopted by some assemblies today are most undignified, and some even infringe on divine principles. Any movement toward a one-man ministry is a movement away from divine simplicity. Paul speaks of himself as *"a minister of the church,"* never as *"the minister of the church."* To quote an old disciple, "Persons are raised up, fitted and gifted by the Lord Himself for His service and work. They are not the product of the world's seats of learning or of human education. We pour no scorn on education, but it cannot of itself make *'a good minister of Jesus Christ'"* (Eph. 4:8-16; Rom. 12:5-8; 1 Cor. 12). Our liberty lies within the sphere of the Word of God and the control of the Spirit. All else leads to bondage. Brethren, let us watch and be sober. "The price of liberty is eternal vigil." The craze for change still rages unabated. Professionalism, intellectualism, organization and centralization, like the four horns of Zechariah 1, are seeking to push the people of God from New Testament simplicity. But God had His carpenters who would build according to the divine pattern. Let us be among the builders. Or to use another illustration, let us seek the grace to be like David's loyal warriors who defended the patch of lentils against all corners, because it was a part of the inheritance of the people of God (2 Sam. 23:11-12).

4. IT IS A FELLOWSHIP OF LOVE

In each of the three chapters that deal with the exercise of gift, humility and love are united. They form the spirit in which our devotions are to move (1 Cor. 12, Rom. 12, 1 Pet. 4). The two tests by which we are to prove our genuineness as the children of God are, *"We know that we have passed from death unto life, because we love the brethren,"* and *"by this shall all men know that ye are My disciples, if ye have love one for the other"* (1 John 3:14; John 13:35). The one confirms our own hearts while the other assures the hearts of others. This is the true Philadelphia ground. The very meaning of the word demands it. This, of course, is not childish sentimentalism which embraces everything and anything. It is *"love in the truth."* It is love to the Lord, to the people of God and love for God's centre. This is the threefold cord that is not easily broken. It will also preserve our fellowship from being broken. John says, *"If we walk in the light as He is in the light, we have fellowship one with another"* (1 John 1:7). In John's first epistle the saints move in the paths of light, life and love. This is because God is light, God is righteous and God is love (1:5, 2:29, 4:16). Hence fellowship with Him is in these three spheres. There is no doubt that one who walks in darkness, who habitually practices unrighteousness and who hates the brethren, is on the line of Cain and not in the family of God at all. He has the spirit of Antichrist and not the Spirit of God. To dwell in God is to dwell in love.

The thought of fellowship is that of partnership or joint- participation. Those jointly sharing are said to be partners (Luke 5:7). It is rendered communion in 1 Cor. 10:16, partakers in 2 Cor. 1:7 and companions in Heb. 10:33. Ours is a fellowship of life, light and love. Christians are not independent units. They are children in one family, members of one body, sheep in one flock, stones in one building, branches in one Vine and sentences in one epistle. The cry of the bride is but the echo of God's dear people in every generation, *"Tell me O Thou whom my soul lovest, where Thou feedest, where Thou makest Thy flock to rest at noon, for why should I be as one that turnest aside"* (or be isolated). God has made us for fellowship. It is the instinct of the new nature to seek our brethren.

5. IT IS A FELLOWSHIP OF LABOUR

A New Testament church has the divine liberty for the exercise of all God-given gift, which includes a variety of gift to meet a variety of need. Since each has his own particular gift, the exercise of that gift will meet a particular need. In 1 Corinthians 3 we have the building and the builders. Paul as a wise master builder laid the foundation for the church at Corinth. He saw the pattern of God's assembly in the laying of the first stone. Other partners in the work are called builders. Paul gives a solemn warning to the builders to be careful of the material they put into the building. Israel built store houses for Pharaoh with wood, hay and stubble. Solomon built God's house with gold, silver and precious stones. What are we building in the light of eternity? Let every man take heed **where** he builds. There is only one foundation. A grasp of this will save us from building on the sinking sands of man's religious organizations. Let every man take heed **how** he builds. It is *"where"* in chapter one, it is *"how"* in chapter two. We can only build in the wisdom of the divine Spirit of God. Let every man take heed **what** he builds (ch. 3). Gold, silver and precious stones refer both to sound doctrine and sound converts. Let every man take heed **why** he builds (ch. 4). Motives must be pure and the Judgement Seat must ever be before us (4:5).

The word *"edify"* means to build. Paul points to the tools the builders are to use: the Word of God (14:3), prayer (14:17), love (8:1) and self-sacrifice (Rom. 15:1,2).

Notice how some of these gifts are designated in 1 Corinthians 3. Ministers or deacons who planted and watered (v. 5) describes the agricultural view of the work. Laying the foundation and superintending the building refer to the architectural aspect of the work. Stewards who fed God's household (4:1), underlings (4:1) who were prepared to do menial tasks in the assembly, fathers (4:15) who graduated from the field of evangelism to the oversight of the flock, all describe the domestic view of the work. Paul says (3:22, 23) all these gifts are yours. The assembly is the only place where there is liberty for the exercise of all God-given gift and where practical manifestation can be given of the principles that are for the whole body of Christ.

In the field of labour everyone of us must remember that we are servants and not a lord among the saints. While Paul gave admonition, he never dictated. Diotrephes dictated, but he never admonished. Paul, the pattern servant, could say, *"Not that we rule over your faith, but are fellow-workmen of your joy"* (2 Cor. 1:24, New Trans.). Distinguished gift, itinerant or local, must ever shun the plague of Nicolaitanism, *"which thing the Lord hates."* Let each of us mind his own business. Let us keep our own place in the Body of Christ and be helpers of the saints' joy, not rulers of their faith,

6. IT IS A FELLOWSHIP OF REPROACH

Christ was put outside the camp by the religious rulers of His day. We are to *"go forth unto Him, without the camp, bearing His reproach."* We cannot abide within, nor can we build up any system of man's religion. In loyalty to Christ and to His Word we must go forth, unto Him, building according to the divine pattern. The cords that bind assemblies together are love to the Lord and devotion to His Word. Our fellowship is not the fellowship of a party, but the fellowship of the Spirit.

7. IT IS A FELLOWSHIP OF THE SPIRIT

We are to endeavor to keep the unity of the Spirit in the bond of peace. The Spirit has already made it; we are to keep it. There are two symbols of the Spirit that express this unity oil and dew (Ps. 133). The unity of the Spirit is good like the oil and pleasant like the dew. That oil was the oil of gladness, sacred, precious and fragrant. The dew was fresh and invigorating like the blessing of the Lord. In what way may the assemblies keep the unity of the Spirit? First, the unity of the Spirit is retained by the reception of the whole Word of God. When we are subject to its authority, allowing it to regulate our whole church life, we shall find joy in that fellowship of light with other assemblies.

Second, the unity of the Spirit is retained by the reception of the people of God. Here, of course, there is spiritual discrimination. We have already pointed out that God has an order in the New Testament: salvation, baptism and reception to the local assembly. But as saints move from place to place they carry a letter of commendation and are to be received as saints. The question arises so often as to what the attitude should be toward assemblies that seem to be determined to link up with the religious world or to copy its ways. Down through the years of assembly history godly brethren have been convinced that a distinction should be made between leaders who lead God's people astray and the sheep of the flock. Leaders who are known to be in the forefront of any movement that is leading the saints away from assembly ground, should be met at the door and kindly told that their influence and teaching are endangering the welfare of the Lord's people. But how often have we seen and heard of godly, humble saints with letters of commendation being turned away for no other reason than that they did not come from the right assembly. Some of these dear souls have been so stumbled and confused by such experiences that their spirits have been broken. Others have been driven back to the sects of men because they saw so little of Christ or Scripture in such procedure. Perhaps brethren who are guilty of these actions may be unconscious of their error. They may even feel they are standing for the truth. But surely the Spirit of God would teach us that to reject a scripturally qualified saint who has already been received in a godly way and who is in good standing in his home assembly, is unchristlike, to say the least. Is there not a guiding principle to govern our attitude and actions in these matters? *"But when ye sin so against the brethren and wound their weak conscience, ye sin against Christ"* (1 Cor. 8:12). Each of us must be on his guard that he does not contribute to a condition of things that would be akin to that described in Third John. Diotrephes, we are told, loved to have the preeminence. It is said that *"he had not seen God."*

How solemn that such a statement should be made by the Spirit of God of a man who held such a position in the assembly. The assembly was in such a condition that it was to be more honourable to be outside in fellowship with John, Gaius and Demetrius, than to be inside with a man who usurped the place of Christ in what used to be *"the church of God which is at Corinth."*

Third, the unity of the Spirit is retained by the reception of accredited servants of Christ. I am speaking now of men who are known for their character and ministry among the assemblies of the Lord's people. Men who have dedicated their lives to the planting of assemblies and the buiding up of the saints in the ways of Cod. It is in such a variety of gift that the assemblies will receive a balanced ministry and be kept from turning to the right hand or to the left. Yet how often has the Spirit of God been grieved by godly servants of Christ, men who have lived for God and His assemblies, being turned down for no other reason than that they will not subscribe to the error of confederacy. Brethren, these things ought not to be. I think I have made it abundantly clear that I am not referring to men who are leading the saints into interdenominationalism or departure of any kind, but men whose character and ministry cannot be challenged.

However, servants of Christ who move in and out of God's assemblies, are not a law unto themselves. Neither should they be beyond the rebuke of their brethren if that is needed. They must be worthy of the confidence of the saints, in dignity, character and ministry. The men whose character and ministry cannot be challenged *"ought to be received"* (3 Jn. 8). Such men belong to all of us (1 Cor. 3:22). To commit the sin of the Corinthians in shutting ourselves up to favourite ministers of Christ, will only lead to the same impoverishment of soul.

I repeat that the assemblies are under no obligation to open their doors to men who are breaking down the line of demarkation between the assemblies and the religious world. Men who are leading the assemblies away from the path of separation and thus forging a link to unite what God has separated, have not earned the right to the confidence of the Lord's people. The pioneers who planted and built up assemblies on this continent were men who saw the errors of denominationalism and taught the saints the same. Yet there are others who would corrupt them with the very errors from which the saints separated when they came out *"unto the Name of the Lord."* May the Lord give us both wisdom and grace to act with clarity of thought and depth of conviction in a day of confusion, and yet with a heart of love for the welfare of all saints.

> Our God is light, and though we go across
>   the trackless wild,
> Our Jesus' footsteps ever show the path for
>   every child.
>
> At every step afresh we prove how sure our
>   Heavenly Guide,
> The faithful and forebearing love that never
>   turns aside.
>
> The manna and the springing well suffice for
>   every need,
> And Eschol's grapes the story tell of where
>   Thy path doth lead.

20

The Unity of the Church

A careful reading of the New Testament will reveal that the unity of the universal church is to have its reflection in the local assembly. There are seven church epistles in the New Testament. These deal with the three great themes of the church and its justification (Romans); the church and its unification (Ephesians); and the church and its glorification (Thessalonians). The other four epistles deal with declension from the first two themes. Ephesians, the central epistle, deals with the oneness of God's masterpiece, the church. Relative to this subject there are two statements emphasized in the epistle: *"the unity of the Spirit"* and *"the unity of the faith."* The first we are to keep for present enjoyment; the other we are to anticipate in its future display. We cannot make this unity. We are simply asked to recognize what the Spirit has already made and will preserve unto the coming of our Lord Jesus Christ — the one, undivided church of the living God,

The truth of the oneness of the church is applied in a practical way to the church at Corinth. Seven metaphors are employed to describe it, with their practical application to the local assembly. These are:

The Church	(1 Cor. 1:2)	unity in our calling
The Vineyard	(1 Cor. 3:9)	unity in our labour
The Temple	(1 Cor. 3:16)	unity in our worship
The Body	(1 Cor. 12:27)	unity in our movements
The Epistle	(2 Cor. 3:3)	unity in our witness
The Family	(2 Cor. 6:18)	unity in our relationships
The Virgin	(2 Car. 11:1-3)	unity of our faithfulness

What precious truths for sweet meditation! The love of the brethren is one of the features of the new creation. It assures our hearts that we belong to Christ (1 John 3:14) and it also assures the hearts of others (John 13:35).

> We love the brethren, Lord; 'tis true because
> in them we see
> Sweet traces of Thy blessed self, for they are
> one with Thee.

Let us look at four aspects of the unity of the people of God. We shall consider it in relation to the cross of Christ, in relation to the words of Christ, in relation to the church of Christ and in relation to the service of Christ.

1. UNITY IN RELATION TO THE CROSS OF CHRIST

Three times in the Word of God we are told that our Lord died so that His people might be one. In John 10:16, 17 we read that the Shepherd was to die that there might be *"one flock and one Shepherd,"* thus indicating a unity of nature and a unity of attraction. Precious indeed is that flock to the heart of Christ. He died for the sheep and makes Himself the joy and satisfaction of each one.

> Our song then forever shall be of the
> Shepherd who gave Himself thus,
> No subject's so glorious as He, no theme so
> affecting to us.

In John 11:52 the high priest of Israel makes a statement that the Spirit of God turns into a prophecy. He said *"that Christ should die . . . that He might gather together in one the children of God that were scattered abroad."* This is unity in relationship — one family and one Father.

Our Lord Jesus, when He thought of the fruit of His death said, *"And I, if I be lifted up from the earth will draw all unto Me."* This is unity of affection One Lord and one Centre. The new nature is created in you and me to find its satisfaction in the triune God. The cross alone could harmonize the attributes of God, bringing God and man together in the bonds of love and union. Now we can sing with joy

> We love the Shepherd's voice,
> His watchful eye shall keep
> Our wand'ring souls among
> The thousands of His sheep;
> He feeds His flock, He calls their names,
> His bosom bears the tender lambs.

2. UNITY IN RELATION TO THE WORDS OF CHRIST

Five times in John 17 our Lord prays that His people may be one. He prays first for that little apostolic band around Him, that they might be one. Then He prays for those who would believe through their word, that they might be one. After that He prays that the whole band of believers may be one. In His high priestly prayer our Lord mentions three things that would maintain this unity unto perfection. First, the power of the Father, *"Holy Father, keep through Thine own Name, those whom Thou hast given Me, that they may be one as We are"* (v. 11). Second, the intercession of the Son, *"Neither pray I for these alone but for them also that shall believe on Me through their words; that they all may be one; as Thou, Father, art in Me, and I in Thee, that they also may be one in Us: that the world may believe that Thou hast sent Me"* (vv. 20, 21). Third, the impartation of His moral glory in the power of the Holy Spirit, *"And the glory which Thou gavest Me I have given them; that they may be one, even as We are one"* (v. 22). Thus the activity of the divine Trinity is operative to bring about the oneness of the Lord's dear people.

It is a unity in separation (v. 11), they are taken out of the world in spirit that they might become the society of heaven on earth. It is a unity in affection (v. 21). The heart has now found its true Object in Christ. The faith of God's elect finds its common Centre in their Lord. It is a unity in holiness (v. 22). The beauty of the Lord Jesus is imparted that it may be reflected.

One day it will be a unity in display (v. 23). Thank God His prayer will be answered. The church universal is one and will remain intact until we are displayed in that unity before the world, at His coming.

> In Him it is ordained to raise a temple to
> Jehovah's praise,
> Composed of all His saints who own no
> Saviour but the Living Stone.
> View the vast building, see it rise, the work
> how great! the plan how wise!
> O wondrous fabric! power unknown that
> rests it on the Living Stone.

3. UNITY IN RELATION TO THE CHURCH OF CHRIST

The unity our Lord prayed for (John 17) is to have a practical manifestation in each local assembly of the Lord's people. Among the sins that needed correction in the church at Corinth, Paul singles out the sin of division first. Its seriousness may be noted in three ways in verse thirteen: It is a sin against the person of Christ, *"Is Christ divided?"* It is a sin against the work of Christ, *"Was Paul crucified for you?"* It is a sin against the name of Christ, *"Were you baptized in the name of Paul?"* What were the sins that marred the reflection of the unity of the Spirit? They were the sins of worldliness, partyism and unchristlikeness. Paul, the spiritual physician among the people of God, having given his diagnosis, prescribes the remedy. For their worldliness he presents the cross of Christ (vv. 17-25); for their partyism he points to the name of Christ (v. 10); for their carnality he ministers Christ in all His sufficiency (v. 30). Thus, Christ, His cross and His name is the medicine of heaven, the healing balm of the leaves from the Tree of Life, for all the sicknesses of His beloved people. Let our souls burn with a holy jealousy for the honour of His name and let us endeavour *"to keep the unity of the Spirit in the bond of peace."*

We will love with tender care, knowing love
    in Christ,
Brethren who His image bear, for the love
    of Christ!
Jesus only shall we know, and our love to all
    shall flow,
In His blood bought church below, for the
    love of Christ.

4. UNITY IN RELATION TO THE SERVICE OF CHRIST

"Behold how good and how pleasant it is for brethren to dwell together in unity" (Ps. 133). It is good in its essence for it flows from the unity of the Godhead. It is pleasant too. It is pleasant to God; He planned it. It is pleasant to Christ; He prayed for it. It is pleasant to the Holy Spirit; He promotes it. It is pleasant to angels; they behold it. It is pleasant to us; we enjoy it. Yea, it is pleasant to the world; it admires it. It is good like the oil and pleasant like the dew. The first describes our unity in worship, inside the veil; the second points to our unity in service, outside the camp. The oil, the symbol of the Holy Spirit, flows from the High Priest to His members below. It is the picture of priestly prerogatives brought into activity in the worship of God.

To all our prayers and praises He adds His
    sweet perfume,
And love the censer raises their odours to
    consume.

No discordant note must ever mar the praise of God. Let this be a warning to any who would dare approach the Lord's table with bitterness in his heart towards others. Malice and envy, like flies in the ointment of the apothecary, destroy the savour of Christ in the soul which should ever be ascending to God in worship and service.

Four things may be noted of this anointing oil.

a. It was precious. Nothing was ever to be made like unto

it. In creating the unity of the church, the Spirit of God made something that cannot be imitated. Man may have his organizations, bound by rules and regulations; God has His unique organism, the church, bound up in the bundle of life.

b. It was sacred. The anointing oil was never to touch the flesh of any man. The movements of the divine Spirit through the members of the body of Christ are spiritual. He will not put His approval on fleshly energy and fleshly activity among His people.

c. It was fragrant. It imparts to the saints the sweet savour of Christ.

> His name shall shed its fragrance still along
>   life's thorny road,
> Shall sweetly smooth the rugged hill that
>   leads me up to God.

d. It was diffusive. It flowed from the head of Aaron to the skirts of his garments. So is the unity of the saints. It flows from the Godhead above to the members of Christ's body beneath. What godly influence spreads from a company of saints, united to Christ and to one another in the bonds of love and union. The unity of God's people is so precious, so sacred, so fragrant that of the seven things God hates, the last and the worst is *"he that soweth discord among brethren"* (Prov. 6:19).

It was pleasant like the dew. From the lofty peak of Hermon the dew was wafted by the wind to the hills of Zion beneath. The vineyards of Zion yielded their fragrance and fruit as the result of Hermon's dew. This is the picture of the saints dwelling together in unity, for whom the Lord commands the blessing, even life forevermore.

> Waft, waft ye winds the story of the Saviour
>   and His love
> As it flows from Godhead glory in celestial
>   heights above;
> We are saved to tell the wonders of
>   redemption that was bought

Through the blood of our dear Kinsman, O
the wonders God has wrought!

But the Spirit flows through channels that are
cleansed by grace alone,
There is music in their witness as His lordship
they do own,
Yet one discordant note will mar a harmony
from heaven,
God give us grace to keep and own what God
Himself has given.

I cannot leave this subject without reminding you of another mountain. It stands out in contrast to the dewy peaks of Hermon. Of Mount Gilboa David raises this lament, "*Ye mountains of Gilboa, let there be no dew nor rain upon you, neither fields of offerings*" (2 Sam. 1:21). Why this song of lament? It was the mountain of division. King Saul was fighting a battle that was not the Lord's. A divided Israel was driven before her enemies and went down in defeat. Let us mark the lesson well. Beloved saints, the Lord is coming soon. Before the Judgement Seat we all must stand. I close with the words of my beloved brother and fellow-labourer, the late Mr. William Bunting:

> Surely the time is ripe to put away all bitterness, to forgive and forget, to renounce the unscriptural practices and worldly innovations which wound the consciences of our brethren and to heal the breaches of past years. In the Lord's Name, let us close our ranks and preserve an unbroken front before an ungodly world that staggers to its doom. 'United we stand, divided we fall.' One can say no more. Will this appeal meet with unresponsive hearts? Shall we admit that our divisions are our shame and then do nothing except continue to blame those from whom we differ? Rather let us arise before it is

too late and put our house in order. May every exercised soul offer earnest and fervent prayer that it may be so.

Let it be rent, the robe of blue,
Its meaning e'er so fair, so true,
Its upper edge, O bind with care,
Its flowing folds, O gird with prayer,
If some would rend, do thou but bind,
And so fulfill the heavenly Mind.
The king declared, 'the case is plain,
The living child cut ye in twain,'
`Ah no!' replied the mother true,
With heart all rent she then withdrew,
She yielded all, the cause was won,
And once again embraced her son;
O yield again! O die anew!
But never rend the robe of blue.
(Ex. 28:31,32; 1 Kgs. 3:16-27)

CPSIA information can be obtained
at www.ICGtesting.com
Printed in the USA
FFOW01n1655060518
46427086-48289FF

9 781926 765150